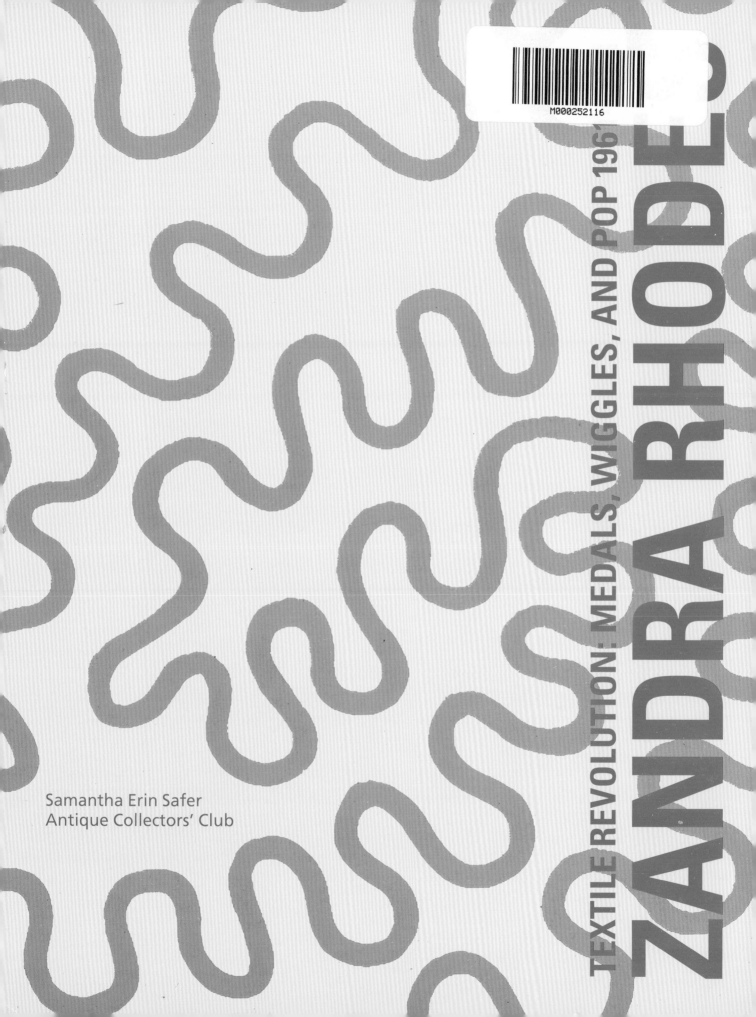

TEXTILE REVOLUTION: MEDALS, WIGGLES, AND POP 196'

ZANDRA RHODES

Samantha Erin Safer
Antique Collectors' Club

TEXTILE REVOLUTION: MEDALS, WIGGLES, AND POP 1961–1971

ZANDRA RHODES

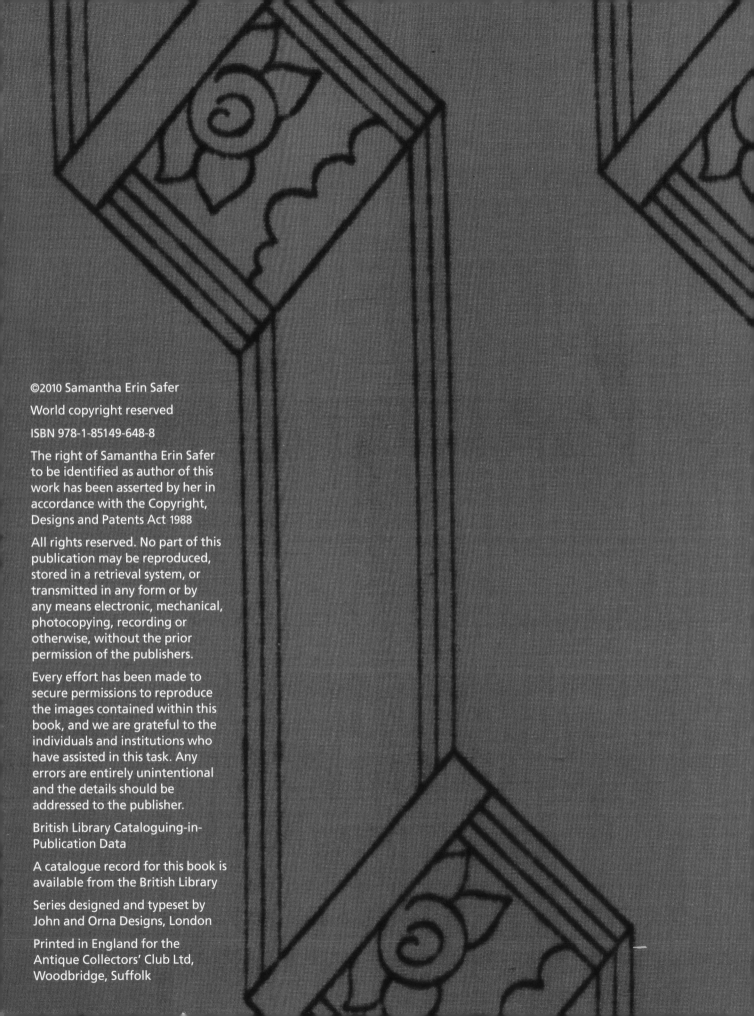

Every effort has been made to secure permissions to reproduce the images contained within this book, and we are grateful to the individuals and institutions who have assisted in this task. Any errors are entirely unintentional and the details should be addressed to the publisher.

British Library Cataloguing-in-Publication Data

A catalogue record for this book is available from the British Library

Series designed and typeset by John and Orna Designs, London

Printed in England for the Antique Collectors' Club Ltd, Woodbridge, Suffolk

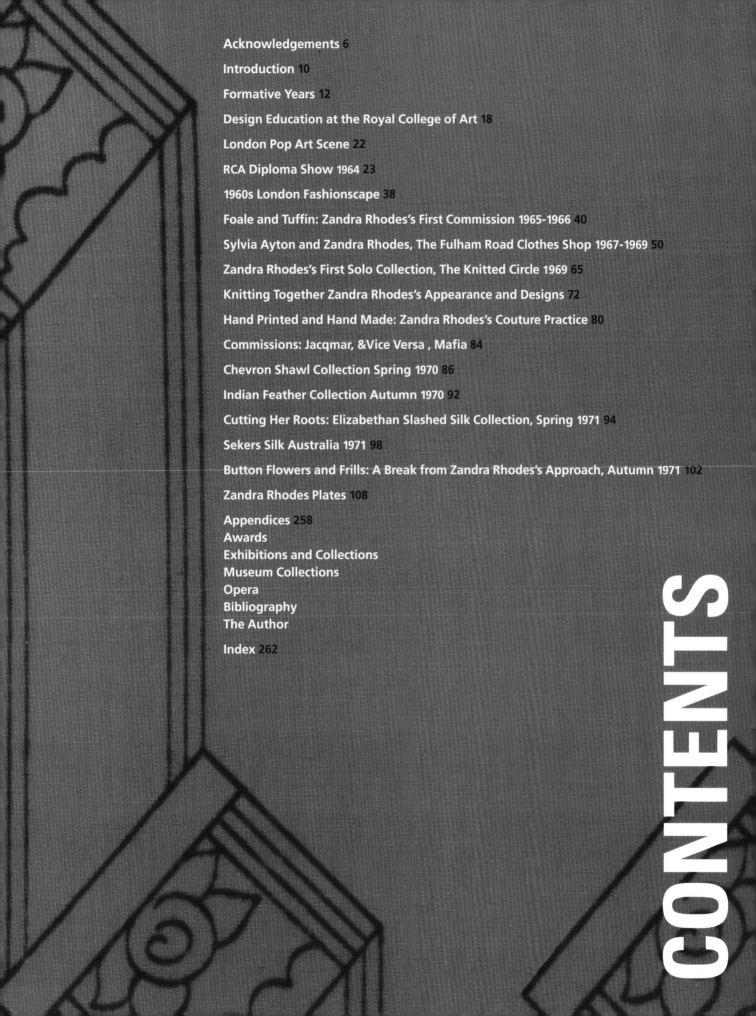

CONTENTS

I cannot begin to thank enough the remarkable Zandra Rhodes, for allowing me the privilege of writing this book on her early work and allowing me unlimited access to her personal archive composed of textiles, dresses, photographs, and press cuttings. Zandra has been beyond generous with her time, talking freely to me about her early textiles and in many ways collaborating on this book; together we have brought to light her previously unseen early work.

This project has been particularly close to my heart. In 2003, I came to London from the States to study and work as an intern at the Fashion and Textile Museum, which Zandra founded, marking the beginning of a close working relationship that has lasted many years. Before I came to London, I had never even heard of Zandra Rhodes, but now this icon of British design has left an indelible mark on my life and career. I remember the first time I stepped into her design studio and was confronted with huge rolls of printed chiffon in every colour imaginable and delicate fantasy-like dresses hanging from dress rails. However, no amount of color and eccentricity could have prepared me for my first sight of Zandra Rhodes in the flesh. She was like nothing I could have imagined. Her hot pink hair was tied up into a topknot, which bore no relationship to the wild hair accessories sticking out from it. She was wearing a full face of make-up on which every color of the rainbow was represented. Staccato lines for eyebrows drawn on with electric blue pencil completed the look. I was at once frightened and in awe of this woman. Her design studio had staff with their heads buried in paper designs, sewing, hand rolling, cutting, and beading her chiffons. Once I'd caught my breath, I felt like I was in heaven. To be asked to write this book on Rhodes's textiles that have continued to inspire me over the years has been an honour. This book would not have been possible without the photography beautifully executed by Patrick Anderson. Thanks extend to Gene Nocon, David Bailey and the other photographers within the book for granting us permission to reproduce their wonderful images bringing Zandra Rhodes's work to life.

Zandra's studio team, particularly all the hard work of her PAs Deborah Ababio in the UK and Cristina Jimenez in the USA, as well as Frances Diplock, Ben Scholten and Kitty Joseph are much appreciated.

Whilst researching this book I have enjoyed many brilliant conversations with Rhodes's closest colleagues and friends allowing me time from their busy schedules to interview them. Particular thanks go to Barbara Brown, Jackie McLennan, Julius Schofeld, Marion Foale, Sally Dennis, Joan Juliet Buck and David Sassoon. Many thanks to Neil Parkinson from the Royal College of Art archive for bringing to light Zandra's early textiles from the college and granting permission to reproduce them here. I also acknowledge the efforts of David Sekers, John Kaldor and Alison Kraus of Angelo Donghia in assisting me to piece together Zandra's early textiles commissions.

I am indebted to Frances Ambler, Anjali Bulley, Teleri Lloyd Jones, and Dennis Nothdruft for the time they took to read the early manuscript and their crack comments, helping

me to work this book into something of which I am fiercely proud. I also extend my thanks to Mark Eastment, V&A Publishing and V&A Enterprises colleagues for their support and encouragement.

Heaps of gratitude to James Smith from ACC, who I can call not only a colleague, but also a friend. It has been a pleasure to work with you on another publication, your generosity of time, honesty, and confidence in my work is dear to me. I would also like to thank Susannah Hecht and the rest of the editorial and production staff at ACC as well as Alison Hart. This book would not have been possible without the photography beautifully executed by Patrick Anderson. Thanks extend to Gene Nocon and the other photographers within the book for granting us permission to reproduce their wonderful images bringing Rhodes's work to life.

Zandra's studio team, particularly all the hard work of her PAs Deborah Ababio and Cristina Jimenez, as well as Frances Diplock, Ben Scholten and Kitty Joseph are much appreciated.

Throughout the years, my dear friends and family have championed my work, cheering me on and lifting me up: Corina Maccarin, Laura Heller, Alexandra Kearse, Dara Heller, Allegra Hirschman, Gity Monsef, Timothy Hunter, Henrietta Fry, Lindsay Harrison, Jessica Kelly, Ellie Herring, Ed Town, the Guttenbergs, Safers, Shaperos, and Zoddas. Finally, I would like to thank my mother, Robin Safer and grandmother, Rita Shapero for their unwavering support in all that I do.

Zandra herself would like to dedicate this book to her partner Salah Hassanein for enabling her to follow her beliefs, Ben Scholten and Chetna Bhatt for their unwavering support and her sister Beverley Haydon.

ACKNOWLEDGEMENTS

Introduction

The education of a young artist, wrote John Ruskin, 'should always be a matter of the head, and heart and hand going together.' Art and design, he said, 'must be produced by the subtlest of all machines which is the human hand. No machine yet contrived, or hereafter contrivable, will ever equal the fine machinery of the human fingers. Thoroughly perfect design is that which proceeds from the heart, that which involves all the emotions; associates these with the head, yet as inferior to the heart; and the hand, yet as inferior to heart and head; and thus brings out the whole person.'[1]

Ruskin could be speaking directly about Zandra Rhodes, British textile and fashion designer, who is world renowned for her fantastically innovative and bright hand-printed designs as well as her own colourful appearance. Exploring Rhodes's treasured personal archive of designs and drawings dating back to the 1950s, her talent, imagination and vibrant creative spirit can be traced throughout. What is apparent is her gift for drawing (the head) and her love for putting ink or paint to paper and fabric (the hand); from lush botanicals and still lifes to outlandish Pop art designs and abstract shapes, they are all rendered with skill and thought (the heart). Known as a prolific draughtsman, Rhodes to this day never travels without her sketch books and is inspired by all that is around her both home and abroad.

By the late 1960s and early 1970s Rhodes won acclaim from the fashion world on both sides of the Atlantic. In 1972, she was named Designer of the Year by the English Fashion Trade with a similar honour, Royal Designer for Industry, bestowed on her in 1974. She was awarded a CBE in 1997. Her intricate and bright textiles, transformed into show-stopping dresses, were splashed across the pages and covers of *Vogue, Harpers Bazaar, Queen, and Women's Wear Daily*. Rhodes's impact, of just one collection from her eponymous line (launched in 1969) was so revolutionary, that her legacy within textile design, as well as fashion, is still felt today. Stars of the fashion world, including John Galliano, Christian Lacroix, Dolce and Gabbana, Mario Testino, Issey Miyake and Manolo Blahnik, all openly cite Rhodes as an inspiration. Lacroix muses,

'Zandra Rhodes contributed to the fashion world like all those who have a radically personal vision…those who innovate and bring the kind of oxygen we need.'[2]

As a young and ambitious textile student in the early 1960s, Rhodes studied at the Royal College of Art (RCA) in London, fertile ground for rising stars in the art, design and fashion world. There Rhodes was exposed to the bold new aesthetic of Pop art. This book investigates Rhodes's early textile designs (1961-1971), many never seen before: from her years at the RCA,

[1] John Ruskin: *The Two Paths, being lectures on art, delivered in 1858-1859*, Maynard Merrill, New York, 1893, Lecture 2, 'The Unity of Art' pp. 54-57.

[2] Christian Lacroix quoted in Gity Monsef, *Zandra Rhodes a Life Long Love Affair with Textiles*, Antique Collectors' Club, 2005, back cover.

[3] Suzy Menkes, *Jewish Chronicle Colour Magazine*, 28 April 1972.

to her first foray into the fashion world with the innovative Swinging London duo Foale and Tuffin, to the launch of her eponymous collection in 1969, as well as her special commissions for Jacqmar, &Vice Versa , Mafia, and Sekers Australia.

Rhodes's early work demonstrates an original approach towards designing textiles, stepping away from the easy, all-over prints popular in the 1930s, '40s and '50s to textiles that are directional, leading fashions within textile design. She plays with colourways as children play with paint, splashing contrasting colours around, adding and taking them away to create a print that, although is the same form, strikes a different note in every colour incarnation. For instance, Rhodes printed *Medals, Bows and Stars* (1964) in twelve colourways using primary colours for bold effects where the bows, stars and brush mark shapes are robust. When printed in softer hues such as light pink, turquoise, white and black, a mellower effect is apparent with the main motifs seeming to collapse into each other. Each collection grows out of her previous ones as she recycles ideas, shapes, and motifs, combining them with new decorative elements. For example, Rhodes is passionate about stitch work and components of stitching appear in all her early textile designs most notably, *Knitted Circle*, *Chevron Shawl*, *Wiggle and Check*, *Sparkle*, *Buttonflower* and later designs from the 1970s and '80s such as *Zig Zag Shell*, *Spinifix Landscape*, and *Torn Square*. Flowers are another idea that Rhodes has built on since 1965. First seen in the form of stylized flowers drawn out of neon-like tubes, her flowers develop sprouting leaves and blossoms in the *Chevron Shawl* print from 1970 and combine with chain-like stitches to form knitted flower shapes in textiles Rhodes designed for Sekers Australia in 1971. A true progression and maturity is gleaned throughout her early work, particularly from her art school years to her first collection in 1969.

Within the realm of fashion design, Rhodes comes out of a tradition of twentieth-century couturiers whose primary concern was with fabric, the construction of the garment being secondary. Designers in this tradition, from Mariano Fortuny and Madame Grés, to Madeleine Vionnet have not necessarily looked to mainstream fashion trends dictated by their respective eras and consequently, have never been in nor out of fashion. Their ultimate goal was to produce individual garments in which the drawing of a textile or the drape of a fabric in relation and to the body remained the first spark of the creative process. This approach was honed at art schools where Rhodes was in constant contact with fashion designers, painters, sculptors, and product designers. As Rhodes's prints are not easy repeats, the intricate flat patterns led her in how she could use them on the body, the silhouettes always being arrived at by experimentation. 'Chiffon – light as air and flying free. Scissored into handkerchief points or folded into intricate pleats. Awash with swirling prints. Glowing with vibrant colour' was how Suzy Menkes described Rhodes's early work in 1972.[3] Zandra Rhodes is a designer who is driven foremost by her individual creativity, which stems, as Ruskin said, from the marriage of hand, heart, and head.

Zandra Lindsey Rhodes was born in Chatham, Kent, England in 1940 where she spent her childhood. She came from a traditional working class family: her father Albert was a lorry driver and her mother Beatrice was a Senior Lecturer on the fashion course at Medway College of Art (now the University for the Creative Arts, Rochester). Prior to her marriage, Beatrice Rhodes had been a fitter at the Worth couture house in Paris and upon her marriage ran a dress making business

designing for private clientele under the old-fashioned moniker Beatrice Modes. Chatham was semi-rural and the family home was a short distance from the picturesque North Downs and woods swathed with bluebells and celandines. One of Rhodes's first drawings for school was the view from the bottom of the garden, looking over the North Downs, scenery she would sketch repeatedly. Rhodes's family life was filled with small town pursuits, going for walks, reading, learning to sew, drawing, and playing with friends. On family holidays they would assemble jigsaw puzzles, the pieces of which would later be reinterpreted into her textile designs as signature wiggles. Rhodes and her sister Beverly were encouraged to do well in school and pursue outside interests. Rhodes openly stated later, that she was

'very boring and snobby. I worked very hard so I was always top. It did not cross my mind whether you liked school or not. I was brought up to believe that if you worked hard, the best person got the job and I was boring enough to not query it.'[4]

With her passion and talent for art and drawing, Rhodes sketched everything from her mother sewing, local people in the market, children, allotments, cabbages, flowers, cathedral doorways to traditional landscapes using a range of materials such as gouache, pencil, pen and india ink. The options for creative young women during the 1940s and 1950s were limited, though this would quickly change in the 1960s. The decorative arts and design provided one of the few areas in which women could become leading, well-regarded professionals. Coupled with the influence of her fashion-designer mother, the natural progression was to pursue a creative yet practical field; however, Rhodes wanted to carve her own path aspiring to become a book illustrator.

After completing O levels at Chatham Technical School for Girls, she achieved A-levels

Right Beatrice Rhodes, Zandra's mother, teaching (second from left, standing)

Opposite Sketch of Beatrice Rhodes sewing from Zandra Rhodes's school sketchbook

[4] *Illustrated London News*, October 1978, Zandra Rhodes Archive.

[5] Zandra Rhodes, interview with author, 14 November 2009.

in History and honours in Art. In 1957, the seventeen-year-old Rhodes entered Medway College of Art as a student in the art department where her mother was lecturing on the fashion course.

"My mother taught dressmaking and I did not want her to teach me at that stage and I did not have a special leaning towards clothing."[5]

Rhodes went to great lengths to keep secret from her peers her mother's tenure at the college, avoiding her as much as possible. At Medway she learnt how to design furnishing fabrics (amongst other media on the foundation course), at the time the main path for textile designers. Rhodes's artistic skill was such that she entered into the second year of the intermediate foundation course, bypassing the first year altogether. After her foundation course, Rhodes studied for a further two years for the National Diploma of Design. Originally,

with the intention of illustration, Rhodes experimented with printing processes on paper such as lino-cutting and lithography in addition to studying printed textiles. Her interest in printed textile design stemmed from the influence of one of her tutors at the college, the innovative textile designer Barbara Brown, who Rhodes greatly admired for her pioneering work and eccentric character. Brown would later become one of Heal's most esteemed designers of the late 1950s and through the 1960s, receiving her first commission straight out of the RCA. Brown lived in London and taught at Medway College of Art two days a week taking the train down to Chatham as many young art graduates did. The Heal's fabric brochure for a new season in 1967 stated 'Barbara Brown has become the golden girl of Heal's fabric designers' and her geometric textile designs, that played with optics and *trompe l'oeil* patterns based on machines and architecture in a large scale perfectly suited the market.[6] Rhodes is passionate about the influence that Brown had on her:

"She was dramatic and exotic with her hair piled up high in a Victorian style and she would wear a Victorian smock for working in the dyeroom. She was very outspoken and told us that if we wanted to study at the Royal College of Art we had to do everything she said. If we did not do our homework, which took the whole weekend, she would ignore us the next week."[7]

Brown educated her students in modern architecture, art, and current textile design and even took them on a trip to Manchester to visit the major printing and dye companies such as ICI, now part of AkzoNobel. Brown drilled into Rhodes the importance of drawing as she felt "drawing is where everything creative stems from" and admittedly "pushed Rhodes very hard" spotting her talent for design.[8] Her impact was such that Rhodes took to wearing a purple smock with lace trim, and Victorian jet jewellery to style herself in Brown's image.

After refocusing her studies on printed textiles in 1959-60, working with colour and mastering it became crucial to her work. A "flamboyantly messy student" always with dye on her finger nails and clothes, she had been captivated by bright colours since a child.[9] Rhodes cites her mother's vibrant and yet glamorous dress sense, as well as Brown's bold textile design, which used colour to a powerful effect, as influences. Striving to derive her own colourways, she took extensive notes on the dyes and formulae for each colour she produced and subsequent combinations of

Above Early gouache sketch of the North Downs by Zandra Rhodes's childhood home in Chatham.

Right Zandra Rhodes sketching in Austria at an early age, It was one of her hobbies.

Opposite *Complex, furnishing fabric,* Barbara Brown, machine screen printed cotton, produced by Heal's, 1967. The strong colour and areas of light and shade give the textile a three-dimensional effect. V&A Images/Victoria and Albert Museum.

6 Heal's fabric brochure 1967.

7 Zandra Rhodes, interview with author, 14 November 2009.

8 Barbara Brown, interview with author, 15 March 2010.

9 Zandra Rhodes, interview with author, 14 November 2009.

10 Zandra Rhodes and Anne Knight, *The Art of Zandra Rhodes*, London, Michael O'Mara Books Limited, 1984, p.11.

colour that created a harmonious, albeit striking, final design. By the mid 1960s brightly coloured and highly complex textile designs were to become Rhodes's signature within the fashion world.

She fell in love with textile design and printing;

'I enjoyed the discipline of the prints that they had to be cut and used economically, that I had to consider measurements and repeats it was both technical and artistic at the same time, and directed towards an end product outside the pattern itself'.[10]

The challenge of textile design was just this: the patterns had to be incorporated into designs of furniture, curtains, clothes, bedding, and other goods co-existing as an elevated art form and mass-produced item. This fuelled Rhodes to explore the depths and possibilities of a pattern. Her creative talent, combined with the technical skills she acquired at college, meant she designed textiles that were not typical all-over repeatable designs, but were directional (one-way or two-way prints) with more painterly qualities. It was at this early stage of her art education that the formation of Rhodes's ideas concerning printed textiles evolved; she considered her prints greater than flat pattern on fabric, and that textile designs should be pieces of art in their own right. On the advice and encouragement of her beloved tutor Barbara Brown, Rhodes applied to the RCA in London; England's pre-eminent postgraduate art school during her final year at Medway in 1960.

Ink drawing with gouache of an
allotment from Zandra Rhodes's
Medway College of Art sketchbook

17

Zandra Rhodes and Alex
MacIntyre circa 1966-67.
The sequin helmet is by James
Wedge and the plastic yellow
suit is Ossie Clark. Courtesy
of Norman Tudgay.

11 Zandra Rhodes, interview with
author, 14 November 2009.

12 Joel Lobenthal, *Radical Rags:
Fashions of the Sixties*, New York,
Abbeville Press Publishers, 1990.
p.14.

13 Christine Bordell, *Horrockses
Fashions*, London, V&A
Publishing, 2010, p. 74.

14 Jacqui McLennan, interview
with author, 1 December 2009.

15 Christopher Frayling and
Claire Catterall, eds, *Design of
the Times: One Hundred Years
of the Royal College of Art*,
Richard Dennis Publications/
Royal College of Art, 1999, p. 73.

16 Lilies first appear in Rhodes's
Lovely Lilies collection of textiles
in 1972. They are comprised
of *Reverse Lily, Field of Lilies,
Lace Mountain,* and *Lilies.*

17 Frayling and Catterall, eds,
p. 73.

18 Lesley Jackson, *Shirley Craven
and Hull Traders: Revolutionary
Fabrics and Furniture 1957-1980*,
Antique Collectors' Club, p.19
& 46.

19 Kodatrace is a transparent
drafting paper made of acetate,
manufactured by Kodak. It was
widely used in the textile
industry for transferring artwork
onto printing screens by creating
'positives' of colour separations.

20 Marnie Fogg, *Boutique: A 60s
Cultural Phenomenon*, London,
Octopus Publishing Group, 2003,
p. 30.

21 Fogg, p. 30.

Rhodes travelled to London and
undertook the pressurized entrance
examination to the RCA, which was spread
over three or four days. The exam demanded
the student draw whilst being observed by the
tutors, and the transformation of drawings into
textile designs. Rhodes also had to undergo
critiques, a lengthy interview, and a review of
her portfolio. There were only six vacancies in
Rhodes's year and she recalls that at least twenty
to thirty people, if not more, applied
for each place.[11] Her hard work paid
off and after dedicating herself to the
examination process, she was not only
rewarded with one of the coveted
places, but she also won a scholarship.

The Butler Education Act of 1944
provided the opportunity for working-
class children and others to enter
further and higher education.[12]
Many students under the act headed
to art college, a new generation
shaking off the 'staid' professional
routes of their parents. Students
received Government subsidies, which
made it possible for an unprecedented
number of students in post-war Britain to pursue
careers in the arts. The RCA was just one of many
institutions that saw an influx of applicants
looking for careers as painters, architects,
ceramicists, and designers of products, textiles,
and new styles. The fashion course at the RCA
was inaugurated in the late 1940s by former
Vogue editor-in-chief Madge Garland, who
placed the programme at the forefront of the
fashion industry during the first half of the
1950s. Her successor, the famous Janey Ironside,
encouraged and motivated the bright young
designers, many of whom rose to prominence
in the 1960s such as David Sassoon, Gina Fratini,
Sylvia Ayton, James Wedge, Angela Sharp, Janice
Wainwright, Ossie Clark, Bill Gibb, Marion Foale
and Sally Tuffin.

A fundamental overhaul of the college
laid the ground to let this talent rise, specifically
in the School of Design. During the 1930s, the
School of Design was greatly criticised for its
emphasis on fine art. A radical transformation
of the school was initiated in 1948 when new
principal, Professor Robin Darwin took up his
post. Darwin divided the School of Design into
smaller specialist schools that included separate
departments for Textile design (Print and
Weave) and Fashion.[13] The new objectives for all
departments in the college were to nourish both
creativity and technical skill with the final aim of
students being employed in industry. It was

crucial to make strong links with industry, and each student in the Textile School had a drawer in the 'plan chest' where their portfolios of design were displayed for buyers from various department stores and textile manufacturers.[14] Mary Oliver, an administrator from the Textile School, looked after the 'plan chest' in the early 1960s and would lead the buyers to certain drawers; both the college and student would make a profit from purchases. This all-important process gave many young textile designers their first foray into the industry. Upon completion of three years' schooling with industry practice in the summer holidays, the student received a DesRCA (Designer of the Royal College of Art) degree. The cross-fertilization of new ideas emerging from the various disciplines within the student body of the college and its staff, led to entirely new approaches to art and design. The staff within the department were the leading lights in design: Peter Rice the renowned theatre and set designer; Bernard Neville of Liberty's print fame; and Professor Roger Nicholson, designer of wallpapers for the Palladio range and fabric designs for the Cotton Board; as well as architect, photographer and designer Humphrey Spender.

Despite its focus on design, the Textile School had yet to realise the potential of fashion as a career path for designers. In fact the word 'fashion' was not uttered within the textile studio until the late 1950s and early 1960s.[15] Sticking to its academic roots, the main pathways were through the design of furnishing fabrics, wallpapers and carpets, not frivolous dress prints. Traditionally, students in their first year were given a fortnight in which to make only calligraphic marks, a week on vertical stripes, another on horizontal stripes, then one on spots and finally six weeks of flower designs. Botanical drawing was still considered extremely important in Rhodes's first year, with tutor Dickie Chopin leading the class, bringing in fresh flowers and plants from Kensington Flower Market for the students to draw as still life studies. Flowers or flower-like shapes were prevalent in Rhodes's early textile designs from her college days onwards; and lilies would become an important motif throughout Rhodes's oeuvre.[16] The designer John Drummond, who was appointed Professor of Textiles in the mid 1950s, assisted in pushing the boundaries of the old guard by encouraging his students away from designing on paper and, by handing them over to print technicians for the final product, towards experiments with the technical side of textile production.[17]

Screen-printing had revolutionised printed textiles in Britain since the war, allowing much greater flexibility and creativity in terms of form, colour, texture and the physicality of scale.[18] The different stages in the screen-printing process, from working out repeats, stops and colour separations, producing kodatraces, to transferring images photographically onto printing screens, mixing dyes and printing fabric were all taught at the college.[19] Rhodes mastered the complicated processes of working out seamless repeats and printing all-over designs. The textile students were taught to be technically sophisticated printers, which gave them an advantage upon graduation. Rhodes's then boyfriend, Alex MacIntyre – a textile designer in his own right – was a highly-skilled screen printer. Upon leaving the RCA in 1964, they set up their own printing studio in West London on Porchester Road, where Rhodes stayed until the 1990s.

The social revolution of the 1960s linked to changes in education, resulting in greater numbers of youth working with disposable incomes utterly transformed culture and economics. Beyond the RCA, London provided a stimulating atmosphere with its exhibitions, music, films, and plays, in which Rhodes could immerse herself. Youth culture in London was making headlines; it was the time of Mary Quant's innovative designs, Vidal Sassoon's geometric haircuts, and the peak of boutique culture. Carnaby Street and the King's Road were already home to trendy shops to which magazine editors and buyers flocked to see the new and youthful fashions. At the RCA, Rhodes was surrounded by a group of young, energetic artists and designers who would emerge as the vanguard of their fields and graduates who played a pronounced role in transforming the aesthetic of the 60s: David Hockney, R.B. Kitaj, Patrick Caulfield, Peter Blake, Pauline Boty, Janice Wainwright, Sally Tuffin, Marion Foale, and James Wedge. Noel Whitcomb in the *Daily Mail* acknowledged the importance of the RCA in fostering such new creative talent,

'It is Britain's university of fashion, a working model of how higher education and industry can go hand in hand for the benefit of all, including the country's export trade. No other country in the world had a state-sponsored fashion nursery like the RCA.'[20]

Marit Allen, editor of 'Young Ideas' in *Vogue* recalls: 'The flux started in 1963, '64. Things started to hot up, young people were finding a new personal voice; they didn't want to be like their parents. There was a new universal movement afoot, that wasn't just about skirt lengths but a new social order. The young didn't want to be part of the existing social structure but wanted to be valued for their own capabilities, enthusiasms, and talent in every possible area. The new designers reflected this.'[21]

Many students recall the buzz of the school and its vibrancy, particularly the importance of the college bar. Other than hosting dances every other week where the students would let loose, it was a space for interdisciplinary interaction between all the students. Jacqui McLennan, a year below Rhodes, remembers how Rhodes would frequently spend time in the Fashion School working with fellow students forming her ideas concerning fashion textiles; her passion did not solely lie with furnishing fabrics. Rhodes worked every conceivable hour she could: the RCA was open twenty-four hours a day, and many of her colleagues thought she slept there.[22] When they arrived at 7am she was already in the studio and always the last to leave late at night, a way of working that is still adhered too. One of Rhodes's legacies would be her prolific design output.

During her second year at the RCA, 1962-3, Rhodes began designing dress fabrics formally turning away from furnishing fabrics. Rhodes muses 'maybe I took to dress fabrics because of my mother? Furnishing fabrics tended to be large-scale, and in the early 1960s, frustrated would-be artists designed furnishing fabrics'.[23] The tutors in the Textile School came to realize that dress fabrics were the bedrock of the fashion industry and the department responded accordingly by building into its syllabus in the 1960s 'visits to fashion houses and the execution of printed and woven fabrics for making up into clothes'.[24] With the increased recognition of dress fabrics and the integration of their design into the curriculum, Rhodes was able to fully explore and develop her ideas for textiles. She was recognized as being something of a maverick within the Textile School as she turned away from furnishing fabrics. Rhodes's initial influences stretched from Salvador Dali and Elsa Schiaparelli's surreal lobster and tear print dresses to the stained glass radiance of Emilio Pucci's prints. "When I was getting really interested in doing dress textiles, Pucci came to London to show his newest collection of giant panel prints and it was a huge influence seeing how someone could do great big colourful textile designs like that."[25]

Artist Sonia Delaunay's approach, conflating textiles, fashion and art, showed Rhodes that she could take disciplines that existed in separate spaces and integrate them. Delaunay freely crossed the borders between fine and applied art giving her clothing the

power and self-assurance of paintings and Rhodes, encouraged by this example, forged ahead with her dress fabrics.[26]

As Rhodes would later explain: 'I was excited by the idea of things divorced from themselves, prints designed flat but never used in that manner. In learning to design for dress fabrics, I was involved in a special adventure, that of patterns which would not hang flat but would be cut and put together again in many different ways.'[27]

Since the textile design would be used in three-dimensions Rhodes had to consider movement when designing. She treated herself similarly 'like a canvas, pinning painted paper designs on to [her]self and walking around, moving, creasing, and studying the effects in the mirror'.[28] The large paper textile designs pinned to her body were influenced by Pucci's large panel prints. It was important for Rhodes to look at the textile in relation to the body to form its arrangement, and acquire a sense of how the textile would move with or against the body. This became a crucial step in designing her textiles and is a method which is still used.

The textiles that Rhodes produced at the RCA were given to her mother, who made them up into dresses, which Rhodes wore with either Roger Vivier platforms (for which she saved earnestly) or Biba boots and bags with rings and other jewellery she bought from Woolworths.[29] Her hair was dramatically dark with a perfectly on trend cut by Vidal Sassoon and she applied very thick black kohl around her eyes accentuated by false eyelashes. Her Professor Robin Darwin joked "Keep death off the Rhodes!" She also wore innovative designs from contemporary fashion students at the RCA:

"I had a purple trouser suit from Foale and Tuffin, I wasn't making my own clothes then, a yellow plastic Ossie Clark suit too and a beloved orange and white coat by Brian Godbold. So I used to go around looking quite amazing. When I went for my driving test the woman had never seen anything like me. She told me it looked terrible and I should take my hat off, in the end she ripped it off. It was a Fair Isle beret from a second hand shop I thought I looked fantastic, so I obviously used to shock then."[30]

Zandra Rhodes's appearance, particularly her style of dressing, was at this time still evolving. She experimented with how far she could push the boundaries of what was acceptable but also how her look could be exploited to court attention and advance her career.

Opposite Zandra Rhodes modelling *Medal Bows* full-length paper panel design. She would paint the full-scale textile design on paper cutting holes in the top of it subsequently trying it on to see how the print looked on the body. *SIA Journal*, No.137, July 1964.

[22] Jacqui McLennan, interview with author, 1 December 2009.

[23] Rhodes, p.12.

[24] Christopher Frayling, *Art and Design: 100 Years at the Royal College of Art*, London, Richard Dennis Publications and Collins & Brown, 1999, p.223.

[25] Zandra Rhodes, interview with author, 14 November 2009.

[26] Elizabeth Marono, *Sonia Deluanay: Art into Fashion*, New York, George Braziller, Inc., 1986, p.8.

[27] Rhodes, p.12.

[28] Rhodes, p.12.

[29] Zandra Rhodes, interview with author, 19 November 2009.

[30] Zandra Rhodes, interview with author, 19 November 2009.

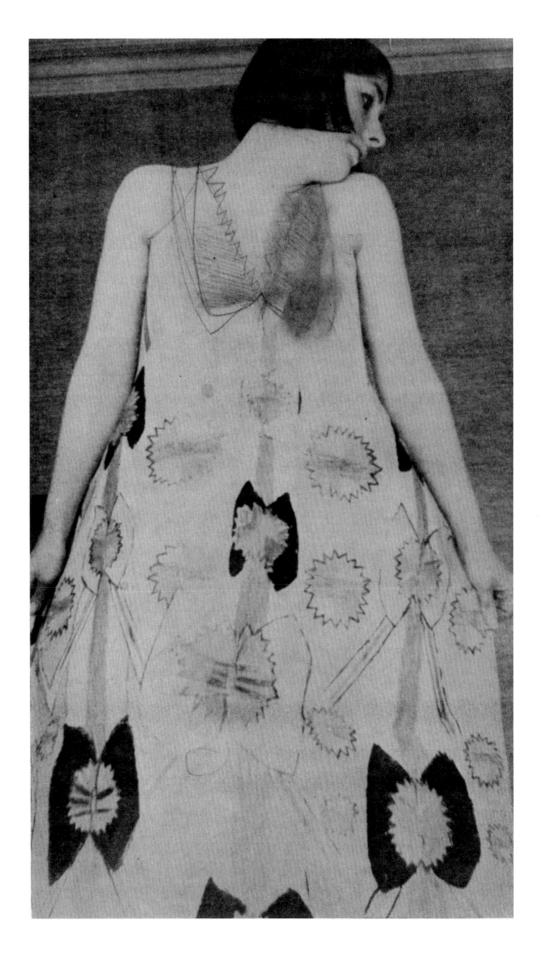

At the RCA, Rhodes's approach was taking fruition as she began to be more comfortable and confident with her method of designing.

"I was influenced by painters such as David Hockney, Andy Warhol, Roy Lichtenstein and what was going on in the painting world and putting that into the textile world."[31]

Pop Art was emerging from the art world in London and New York during the late '50s and early '60s, stemming from 'low culture' sources of inspiration such as print advertisements, comics, television, and other forms of mass culture. In 1957, leading Pop artist Richard Hamilton spelt out the new criteria for Pop Art:

'Popular (designed for a mass audience), Transient (short-term solution), Expendable (Easily forgotten), Low cost, Mass produced, Young (aimed at youth), Witty, Sexy, Gimmicky, Glamorous, Big business.'[32]

In London, the painting scene was flourishing with new vibrant artists working within the Pop idiom; David Sylvester at the time explained that Pop Art

'incorporates into "fine art" things that ordinary people are interested in looking at, makes us look at them again in a new way.'[33]

This new way of looking and interpreting culture was widely apparent in the *Young Contemporaries* exhibition, an annual juried affair showcasing works from art schools throughout Britain. The work exhibited brought into focus the new generation of painters from the RCA demonstrating this new easy to look at aesthetic that used a common visual language. The documentary film by Ken Russell, *Pop Goes the Easel* shown in March 1962 on the BBC's *Monitor*, went further in attempting to define the emerging Pop movement in Britain. The film followed four artists, Pauline Boty, Peter Blake, Derek Boshier and Peter Phillips, identifying them as the new artistic movement giving British Pop art legitimacy with the general public.[34]

Rhodes wanted to take her artistic ideas into the larger realm of fashion, encouraged by the collapse of the barriers between artists and designers, not only within the environment of the RCA, but within wider industry and culture. The example of these shifting territories was directly related to the breakdown between one-off designs and mass-produced products and the Pop movement coursing through the RCA. The old divisions between art and industry, craft and design suddenly became irrelevant. Pop made everything 'commercial'. Commercial art became fine art and translated itself into textiles.

Zandra Rhodes's diploma show in 1964, or as it was called at the RCA 'The Major Task', was the confluence of every idea she had concerning dress textiles, their possibilities and art. She showed twelve hand-printed textile lengths, seven designs in one colourway, three designs in two different colourways (*Flags, Comic,* and *Starburst*) and two further designs in three colourways (*Medals, Bows and Stars* and *Spiral Flowers*) in floor to ceiling lengths of cloth, as was the traditional mode of display for the Textile School. In front of the panels on tables were smaller printed swatches, paper artwork of the designs, sketchbooks, preliminary research showing her complete design process and studies of the particular motifs such as medals, grosgrain ribbon, and stars that were pinned to the wall. Inspired by Roy Lichtenstein and his comic book style, Andy Warhol's *Soup Cans*, Jasper John's flag paintings and David Hockney's early work, Rhodes produced fresh vibrant textile designs.

During the summer holidays before the final year preceding the Diploma Show, the textile students were briefed and set their 'Major Task'. Rhodes chose medals as her theme and the work was all grounded in the Pop idiom. The *Medal Series* (composed of four prints: *Medals; Medals, Bows and Stars; Medal Bows;* and *Medal Ribbon Check*) was influenced by the work of former RCA painting student David Hockney, (a third-year student when Rhodes was a first year) particularly his painting, *A Grand Procession of Dignitaries* painted in the Semi-Egyptian style from 1961. This featured little medal-like shapes along the border as well as decoration on the Egyptian style figures dressed in cloaks.

"From the way the picture was created it was the medals that first caught my eye" said Rhodes.[35]

[31] Zandra Rhodes, interview with author 19 November 2009.

[32] Hamilton wrote a note to the brutalist architects Alison and Peter Smithson, who had contributed to *This Is Tomorrow* the Independent Group's historic exhibition at the Whitechapel Gallery in London. The note discussed the idea of a subsequent exhibition with a similar theme. It was in this note that Hamilton coined the phrase pop art and then described it using the quote above.

[33] David Sylvester, 'Dark Sunlight', *Sunday Times Colour Supplement*, 2 June 1963, pp. 3-14.

[34] David E. Brauer [*et.al*] *Pop Art: US/UK connections, 1956-1966*, Houston, Texas, Menil Collection, 2001, p. 65.

[35] Zandra Rhodes, interview with author, 14 November 2009

With this theme in mind, Rhodes researched the various shapes and sizes of medals, sketching examples on view at the Imperial War Museum and Wellington Museum, taking in the coloured grosgrain ribbons that hung from them, even going a step further and deconstructing the grain of the ribbon in her prints. The stars and bows added to the medal designs were influenced by military portraiture. These motifs were all translated into designs with bright Pop colours, energetic shapes, and a sophisticated yet childlike positive energy. Ironically, the print *Medals* was bought by Heal's from Rhodes's Diploma Show and produced as a furnishing fabric entitled *Top Brass*.

The *Medal Series* enabled Rhodes to experiment with various printing techniques,

A Grand Procession of Dignitaries painted in Semi-Egyptian style, David Hockney, Oil on Canvas, 1961, Courtesy of David Hockney. The medals running along the top border of the painting and those hung on the figures' cloaks inspired Rhodes to concentrate her diploma collection of textiles on the theme of medals.

Top Brass, eight-colour print on cotton sateen produced as a furnishing fabric for Heal's, displayed in Zandra Rhodes's diploma show at the RCA, 1964.

25

This and following spread
Four images from Zandra
Rhodes's RCA Diploma Show,
July 1964, ©Royal College
of Art.

screens, and colours. *Medals*, for instance, was an eight-colour print that used the reciprocal number of screens; whereas for *Medals, Bows and Stars*, Rhodes tested a discharge printing

technique (where the colour is bleached out) in violet and white, black and white, as well as trialling twelve different colourways printed on to swatches. She states, 'I like garish colours – the things people call a bit too bright. If colours always "go" together, it will always have to be Swedish design, and you don't want that, do you? Sometimes you walk through the Design Centre and everything's so tasteful. I don't want my things to be all tasteful and beautiful. I can't bear good taste.'[36] Rhodes used acid dyes to print with as they kept a richness and good depth within the fabric and were the best dyes for silk, a material commonly used by Rhodes. Additionally, acid dyes worked well for making many bright and garish colours sit and overlay together on the fabric.

Rhodes also visited exhibitions at the famous museums and contemporary art galleries around London and furiously sketched anything that interested her. Back in the textile studio, Rhodes would re-arrange her sketches and ideas cutting into them, pasting them back together, and re-drawing them into designs or little studies until they were worked up into complete full-length garment panels. The panels, especially those from the *Medal Series* owe a nod to Pucci's panel prints, which featured in popular fashion magazines in the mid-1960s during the fashion house's prime. The full-length repeat panels that Rhodes featured in the Diploma show fulfilled her goal of moving away from furnishing fabrics and into the uncharted territory of fashion textiles. A writer for the *Society of Industrial Artists Journal* who visited the show commented,

'Zandra Rhodes, for instance, is conceiving printed dress fabrics in an entirely different way: not as small repeats which can be cut at will by fashion designers, but in repeat lengths which make up into a complete garment. Some of her designs and colourways are outstanding, and even though they are in large repeats, they have no visual connections with furnishing fabrics.'[37]

Other outstanding dress prints featured in the show were *Dots and Explosions*, heavily influenced by comics (such as *The Dandy*) crudely printed in black and red half-tone dots that Rhodes purchased from her local newsagents as well as Roy Lichtenstein's painted interpretations of American comics with their over-blown aesthetic. The explosions were inspired by the large word bubbles featured in the comics

Top *Comic*, four colour print on calico, displayed in Zandra Rhodes's diploma show, 1964. The print was based on comics Rhodes purchased from her local newsagent like *The Dandy* and Roy Lichtenstein's paintings with half-tone dots and word bubbles reinterpreted into explosions.

Opposite Crayon Study of Medals on paper, RCA, 1964.

[36] *Sunday Times Magazine*, 30 August 1964, p.44.

[37] *Society of Industrial Artists Journal*, Number 137, July 1964, p.2.

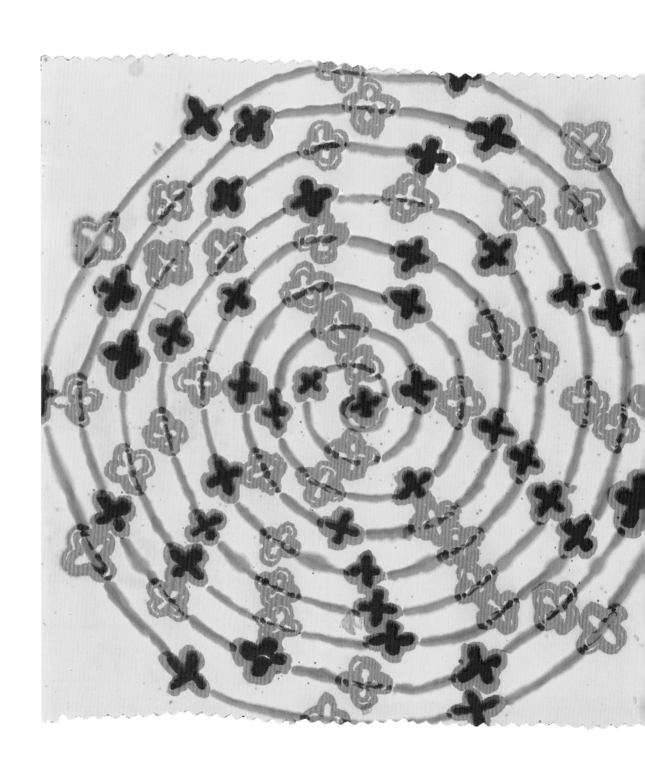

Spiral Flowers, four-colour discharge print on yellow silk twill, displayed in Zandra Rhodes's diploma show at the RCA, 1964.

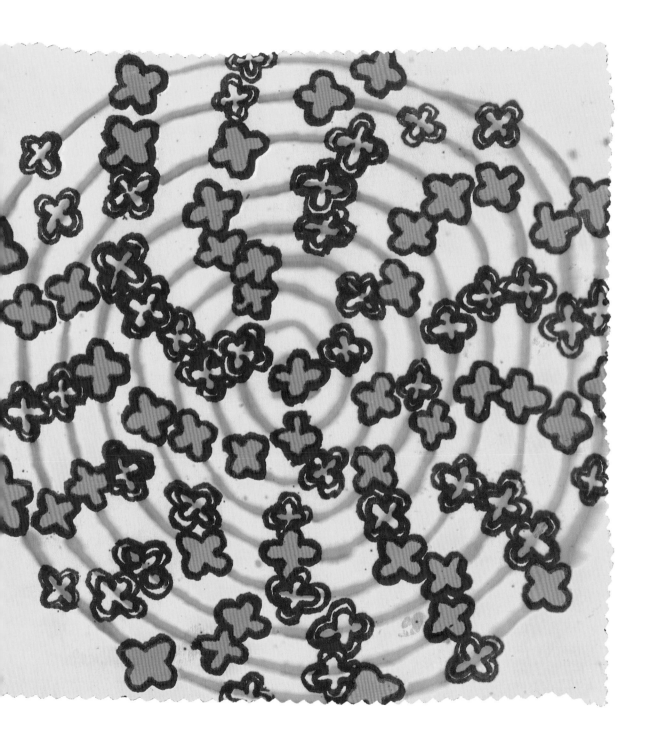

Below Zandra Rhodes wearing a dress of *Spiral Flowers* print, which was made by her mother. This photograph was featured in the *Sunday Times Magazine* on the 30 August 1964 with an accompanying article on the recent RCA graduates.

Opposite, top Iznik bowl, Turkey 1545-50. V&A Images/ Victoria and Albert Museum

Opposite, bottom left *Mr Man*, three colour print on rayon crepe, Sylvia Ayton and Zandra Rhodes, 1968.

Opposite, bottom right Omo Soap advertisement which inspired Rhodes's *Mr Man* print.

38 Rhodes, p. 16.

and dead firework packets found lying on the ground after Guy Fawkes Night. Rhodes produced her own designs in a manner that was suitable for textiles with enlarged red and black half-tone dots and exaggerated to a point of distorted explosions in an all over pattern.

Another comic style illustration pasted into one of Rhodes's sketchbooks featured a swirling explosion with little stars and a Turkish Iznik bowl. The sixteenth century vase, from the Victoria and Albert Museum (V&A) ceramics collection, had a similar loosely circular decorative design and was the initial starting points for the *Spiral Flowers* print. The textile was printed in three different colourways for the diploma show; purple, pink, green and blue on yellow cloth; pink, green, yellow and purple on black cloth; as well as black, on white cloth.

Spiral Flowers was another print where Rhodes played with colour combinations printing up to ten different swatches before selecting the strongest to be exhibited. Rhodes's *Flag* textile designed in 1962 has its origins in Jasper Johns's series of flag paintings and the use of the Union Jack within London's Pop Art scene. It was translated into a chubby flower shape in electric colours on a vibrant yellow ground and was used by Ossie Clark for one of his garments in his first year student show.

Other latterly important designs from 1962-4, *Lightbulbs* and *Mr Man*, which were not featured in Rhodes's diploma show but began their incubation whilst she was studying at the RCA. Being short of money as a student, Rhodes's lifestyle was simple and centered on textile design, printing, television, the supermarket and any trips within her and her boyfriend's means. At the time, Jonathan Miller, editor and presenter of the BBC's television arts programme, *Monitor*, aired a vivid documentary on Las Vegas featuring the gloriously kitsch neon signs and 'electric sculptures of light bulbs in the sky' as Rhodes called them. The Neon Man (the famous Las Vegas signpost figure of a cowboy towering over the old town) advertising the programme on the cover of the *Radio Times* greatly inspired her.[38] This, combined with the packaging of OMO soap powder (advertisements were posted through Rhodes's letterbox consequently she used OMO to wash her clothes), which featured men in rainbow suits and the famous Blackpool Illuminations, served as inspiration. As a result spectacular magical fountains made from coloured bulbs found their way into her sketchbooks. Rhodes started drawing light bulbs, neon tubes, light filaments, and shaped tube lights creating a colourful and intricate *Lightbulb* print. Building on the original print, Rhodes added the motif of men to create the five colour *Mr Man* design, a highly complex pattern that recalled the live sparkling and blinking light filaments from the Illuminations. These prints would later be developed and brought to life in the designs of Rhodes's own line with Sylvia Ayton and the Fulham Road Clothes Shop.

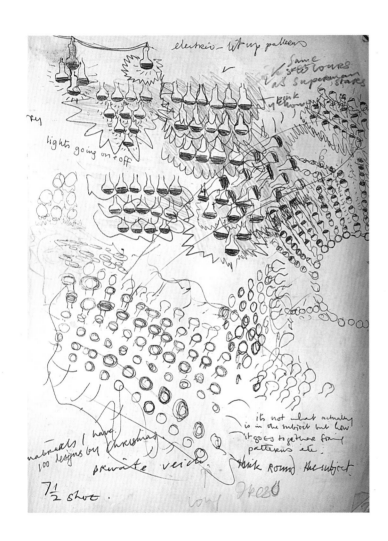

A page of Zandra Rhodes's sketchbook featuring light bulb clusters drawn at the Blackpool Illuminations. The clusters of light bulbs from this sketch are seen in the final textile design.

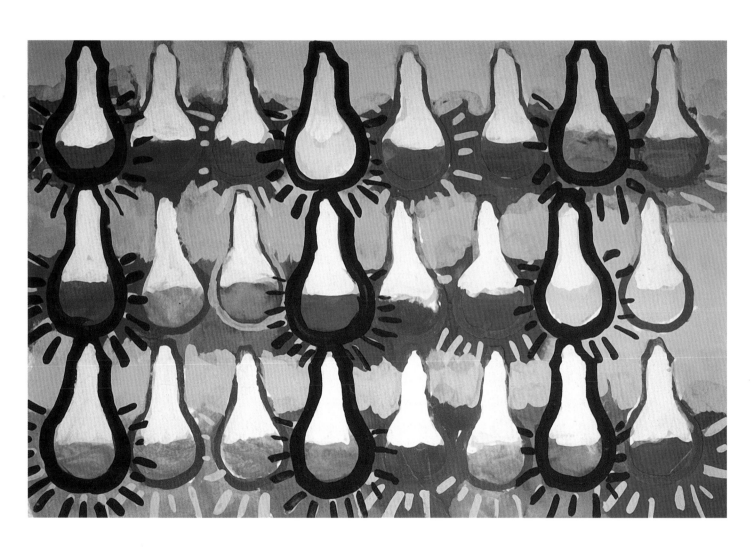

Lightbulb paper design, 1967.
Zandra Rhodes commented
that there were far too many
colours to be practical for
production.

The peak of the post-war baby boom in Britain in 1947 meant that unparalleled numbers of teenagers reached puberty in the 1960s and would achieve a greater influence on society than in previous generations. Youth questioned their parent's values and rebelled against them, basking in a loosening of tradition in many aspects of society. In 1956, there were five million teenagers in Britain, four million of them working.[39] With their independent incomes, teenagers and young adults were more able to pay for the lifestyles they wanted purchasing clothes, music, cosmetics, and accessories. For an aspiringly fashionable youth in London, the two places to hang out and purchase reasonably priced ready-to-wear were Carnaby Street in Soho and the King's Road in Chelsea. A new breed of British 'dolly bird' fashion designers and working-class lads, the likes of Mary Quant, Barbara Hulanicki at Biba, Foale and Tuffin, Gerald McCann, Bill Gibb, David Sassoon, Kiki Byrne, Alice Pollock, Jean Muir at Jane and Jane, John Bates and Caroline Charles were designing precisely for themselves and their friends; for the first time breaking the class barrier in couture. They were the antithesis of Mayfair couture houses and Savile Row – the new arbiters of style. Many of these designers had been educated in the fashion and textile departments of the country's art schools; the newcomers were refreshingly unconventional. They completely rejected the look of Parisian *haute couture* aimed at a wealthy, mature client, instead striving for an immediate and ever-changing fashion aesthetic. Janey Ironside, Head of the Fashion Department at the RCA in the 1960s recalls,

'The students did not like the couture or what it stood for; they were nearly all working-class and had never known the life they saw pictured in *Vogue*.'[40]

Men and women delighted in their youth and craved clothes that reflected this feeling. Freedom of expression reigned; therefore, shopping involved not only the purchasing of clothes and their accessories but became a means of identification with the burgeoning sub-cultures of the time. Shopping for fashionable clothes became central to the experience of being young, attractive, and cool; clothes were a password to a chosen set.

'At the moment,' Georgina Howell declared in the *Observer* in January 1966, 'London is the only place where anybody can wear anything they like and get away with it.'[41]

Of the new designers who trained at these art schools, Mary Quant was the first and most influential designer, her example paving

the way for generations to come. In 1955, on the King's Road, Quant opened Bazaar, the first boutique that catered exclusively for an emerging youth market. A brilliant businesswoman, articulate in her ideas, Quant led the fashion rebellion against couture dominance.[42] She made fun, easy-to-wear, and classless clothes. The designs based on simple, slightly flared child-like shift shapes and tubular lines pitching waists at a low level, used horizontal bands and triangular insets of pleats at the hemline to permit maximum movement. She accessorized her outfits with PVC boots and thick coloured tights. Quant's success encouraged other art-school trained designers to try their hand in opening boutiques or creating their own independent lines instead of the traditional career route (of being dependent) working for a large manufacturer.

A new type of media consumption in the form of magazines, along with a fresh breed of stylish fashion editors, assisted in disseminating what and who was fashionable. The first colour supplement magazine accompanied the *Sunday Times* newspaper in February 1962, this was followed by the *Telegraph* in 1964 and *Observer* a year later. *Queen* magazine had undergone a modern rejuvenation adding the 'About 20' pages (targeting the newly found twenty something market) and the newly launched *Nova* magazine had one sole agenda – to push the boundaries of publishing. The fashion editors such as Marit Allen (*Queen* and later *Vogue* from 1964 onwards), Caterine Milinaire (*Queen*), Sandy Boler (*Vogue*), Meriel McCooney and Brigid Keenan (*Sunday Times*), Felicity Green (*Daily Mirror*), Molly Parkin and Caroline Baker (*Nova*), fastidiously researched the most happening designers going from studio to studio, promoting the talented designer's work and propelling them to stardom. They were bright young things themselves and interested in bright young things.

Zandra Rhodes in her London flat with friends including Janet Street-Porter and Kansai Yamamoto circa 1971, Courtesy of Tim Street-Porter.

[39] In Britain, a young secretary or hairdresser earned 12 to 15 pounds a week by the mid-sixties and the very fashion conscious would spend half of that on the new fashions. From Jane Mulvagh and Valerie Mendes, *Vogue History of 20th Century Fashion*, London, Viking, 1988, p. 238.

[40] Janey Ironside quoted in Mulvagh and Mendes, p. 239.

[41] Georgina Howell, *The Observer*, January 1966, quoted in Lobenthal, p. 30.

[42] Mulvagh and Mendes, p. 239

Zandra Rhodes graduated from the RCA in 1964 and struggled to find a market for her dress fabrics, as there were not many outlets that would purchase inventive Pop style textiles. She interviewed with Emilio Pucci who was in London making an appearance at Woollands Department store in Knightsbridge, London in 1964. He did not offer Rhodes a job, instead suggesting she work to execute her designs in black and white. She now looks back at this memory with laughter, though at the time felt crushed by someone she had been so inspired by.

Her tutors at the RCA thought he might have offered her a job in his Italian studios. Rhodes then tried the more traditional textile route of selling paper designs to large fabric companies. Fabric wholesalers and other large textile firms from Manchester and other parts of the country complained that her prints were too bold, colorful, and inventive; the over-arching consensus was her textiles were "too extreme".[43] Unable to break into the mainstream market, Rhodes and Alex MacIntyre, Rhodes's then boyfriend, decided to establish a textile printing business in their studio on Porchester Road, buying equipment, where she could print her own designs and sell them direct to the young fashion designers in London. In addition to Rhodes's prints, they took on other textile designers' printing to help pay the bills. Rhodes also taught textile design two days a week at Ravensbourne College of Art in Kent where artists like Paul Huxley and designers James Wedge and Sylvia Ayton also taught, and with whom she would later go into business.

Rhodes's first success was with Marion Foale and Sally Tuffin, the designers behind the trailblazing Foale and Tuffin label. Both RCA graduates, they launched their label in 1961, straight out of college, selling to Woollands 21 Shop as well as Paraphernalia in New York. They subsequently opened one of the most successful women's boutiques on Carnaby Street in 1965. They designed quirky trouser suits, dresses, and accessories; and with the likes of David Bailey photographing their work for *Vogue*, and Cathy McGowan wearing them on *Ready, Steady, Go!* they changed attitudes of what young design students could accomplish as independent designers.

Opposite, left *Stars*, two-colour print on rayon crepe for Foale and Tuffin, 1964.

Opposite, right Jane Best models Foale and Tuffin trouser suit in *Star* print, designed by Zandra Rhodes, 1964, Rick Best.

Right *Starburst*, three-colour print on yellow wool challis, displayed in Zandra Rhodes's diploma show at the RCA in 1964. This print was produced for Rhodes's first collection of textiles for design duo Foale and Tuffin in 1965.

[43] Zandra Rhodes, interview with author, 19 November 2009.

Cover of *Queen*, December 1964. Jill Kennington models Foale and Tuffin's trouser suit in Zandra Rhodes's *Star Trellis* print, which featured in her RCA diploma show, 1964.

Left Cover of *Queen*, December 1964. Jill Kennington models Foale and Tuffin's trouser suit in Zandra Rhodes's *Star Trellis* print, which featured in her RCA diploma show, 1964. This was Rhodes's first magazine cover.

Opposite *Stars*, two-colour print on rayon crepe for Foale and Tuffin, 1964.

Below *Stars* paper design composed of gold stars and paint on shiny paper, RCA circa 1962-3.

Opposite *Dominoes* print by Zandra Rhodes for Foale and Tuffin. The trousers sold for 6 guineas in Foale and Tuffin's Carnaby Street shop in 1964.

44 Marion Foale quoted in Iain R. Webb, *Foale and Tuffin: The Sixties. A Decade in Fashion*, ACC Editions, 2009, p.139.

45 Sally Tuffin quoted in Webb, p.139.

As Marion Foale remembers:

"[Zandra's] first job was with us. That is how she got started. We were still on our one floor above Marlborough Court, and she'd just left college [a few years] after us and came to us wanting to sell her prints to people that made clothes, and could we look at them, and we did."[44]

"The first time Zandra came with her prints" recalls Sally Tuffin, "she came with a big piece of [printed] paper with a hole in the top and she just put it over her head. And it fitted. We did quite a lot with her. The photograph of Janey Best wearing the *Star* print, which was taken by Janey's brother, that was a Zandra Rhodes print."[45]

Rhodes was granted a scholarship to travel after graduating from the RCA but forewent it to work printing the textile designs required by Foale and Tuffin. Three of the designs chosen for her first collection with the young duo were from her diploma show, *Star Trellis*, *Medal Bows* and *Starburst*; printed on lightweight wool challis. Unusually, as well as the Foale and Tuffin label, a separate label denoting that Zandra Rhodes had designed the print was sewn into the garments, a clever tool used to promote her designs. For *Starburst*, Rhodes distorted the stars creating spiky circles and colourful baseball-inspired shapes on yellow wool. Other designs from the first collection printed on satin and crepe were a variation on the star theme. *Stars* had featured heavily in the *Medal Series* of diploma prints; *Medals*, *Bows* and *Stars*, *Star Trellis*, and star-like shapes were used in *Spiral Flowers*.

The *Star* print here was the first print created specifically for Foale and Tuffin in 1964. It reinterpreted the motif in a simplified repeat using patriotic colours of red, white, and blue, following the current fashion of using the Union Jack, a key symbol in much '60s London fashion.

The first collection was troublesome to produce; it was almost impossible to print pigment on wool; Foale and Tuffin were keen to

have this fabric. Rhodes chose to print on the fabric using acid dyes with a technique of steaming and washing for finishing the dye process. With some assistance from the textile technicians at the RCA, they put Rhodes in touch with Ivo Prints, a London converter, making it possible for Rhodes to succeed in delivering her first collection. In December 1964, just months after graduation Rhodes had landed her first magazine cover, a dream of all designers. *Queen* featured the *Star Trellis* print, which Foale and Tuffin made up into a brilliant long sleeved trouser suit modelled by Jill Kennington.

Their way of working together would see Rhodes go along to Foale

Next page left Halter neck crepe jumpsuit with Zandra Rhodes's *Zigzag Medal Bows* print, 1965, Helmut Newton/Vogue ©The Condé Nast Publications Ltd.

Next page right Crepe skirt in Zandra Rhodes's *Rainbow* print, 1965, Helmut Newton/Vogue ©The Condé Nast Publications Ltd.

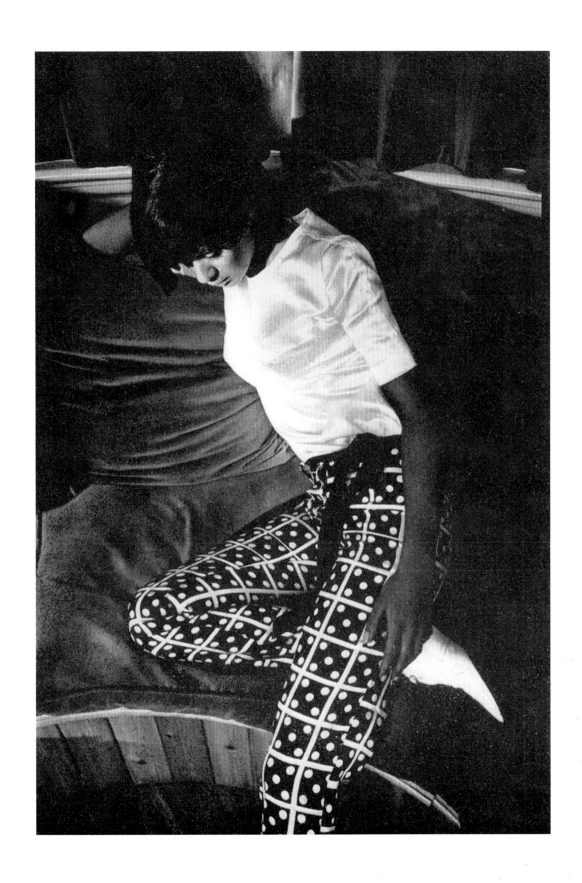

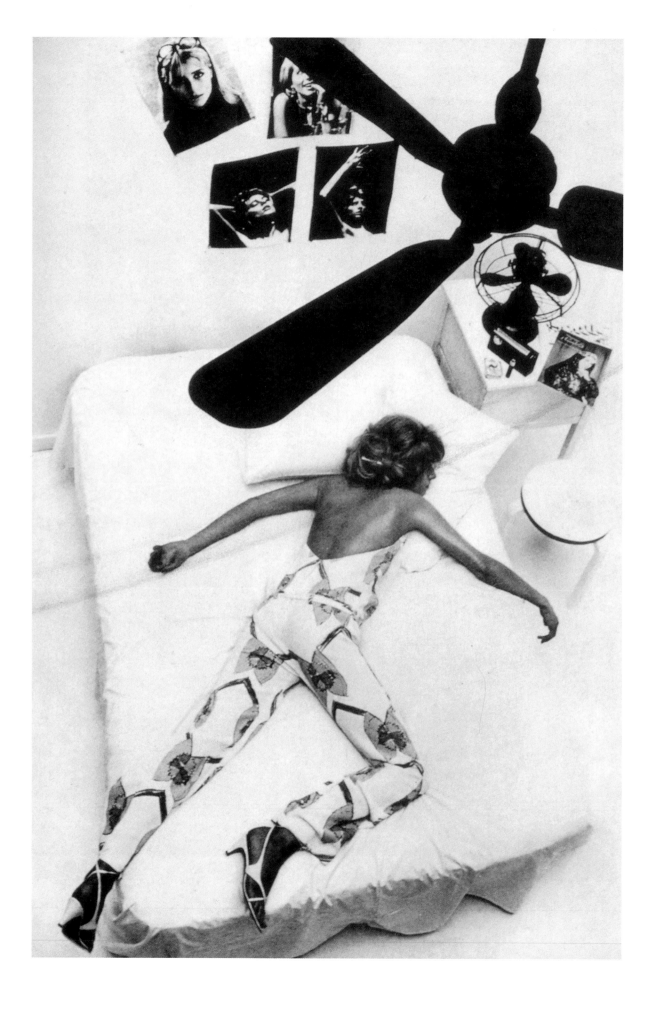

Zandra Rhodes   32 St Stephens Gardens   London W2   BAYswater 1703

Design; Rainbow
(from Vogue July 1965)

and Tuffin's studio with her textile designs and they would choose designs, sometimes suggesting amendments to them. Rhodes's second collection featured more abstract Op Art prints in black and white printed on satin resulting in the prints *Step Up Stars* and *Dominoes*, which were used for bold trousers, blouses and skirts, to striking effect. The third and final series of textile designs in 1965 were *Rainbow* and *Medal Bows,* printed on crepe, the latter created at the RCA. This collection of prints for Foale and Tuffin resulted in the collaboration of work being featured in *Vogue,* with a model wearing a halterneck jumpsuit, in *Medal Bows* print and in another image, a knee-length skirt in *Rainbow* print photographed by Helmut Newton. The appearance in a large fashion spread was the perfect finale for Rhodes and Foale and Tuffin's design relationship to end on.

Rhodes was becoming increasingly disgruntled at selling her textiles direct to designers and not having an input into how they were used.

'I was unhappy that my patterns were just being cut out at random and the possibilities of what the print and the garment could do together were being ignored.'[46]

Marion Foale concurs, "Zandra always had very strong ideas of her own and was not one for bending too far – just like us in fact! We went on with that until she felt she wanted us to do the designs of the garments as she wanted them designed and we said perhaps it is time for you to do it yourself."[47] Rhodes did exactly this with fashion designer Sylvia Ayton, a close colleague from Ravensbourne College of Art. Ayton was also a dear friend of both Foale and Tuffin, having studied with them at Walthamstow Art School and then at the RCA. Rhodes and Ayton planned a collection together called Sylvia Ayton and Zandra Rhodes, Rhodes creating the textiles whilst Ayton designed the clothes. They sold their designs wholesale and later opened the Fulham Road Clothes Shop.

Foale and Tuffin's crepe party pyjamas in Zandra Rhodes's *Rainbow* print featured in advertisement for trendy New York boutique Paraphernalia.

[46] Rhodes, p.16.

[47] Marion Foale, interview with author, 21 December 2009 and Webb, p.139.

ANGLOMANIA
ANGLOMANIA
ANGLOMANIA
ANGLOMANIA
ANGLOMANIA
ANGLOMANIA
ANGLOMANIA
ANGLOMANIA

It all began with the Modness that started a few years back in Chelsea. Now the mania for young English fashion is here, there, everywhere. Anglomania's spread to the staidest department stores, but it literally runs rampant in tiny, special boutiques. London has whole blockfuls of them (over there, they call them "bous"), and a new one's just opened in New York. Devoted to fledgling designers both Anglo and American, Paraphernalia's run by Susan Burden (one of June MLLE's Young Smarties), who also models for the shop, assisted by ex-MLLE staffer Betsey Johnson, who also designs for the shop. . . . This page: Party pajamas, part siren slither, part boop-boop-a-doop, all black-and-white-squiggled crepe. By Foale & Tuffin, about $55. That's Susan Burden, Paraphernalia's model-cum-manager. Her funny, bowed black silk shoes, VanEli. Opposite: Flannel to the floor, the bodice just three buttons deep, the sleeves sheer (i.e., organdy) seduction. By Mary Quant, pale-blue wool, about $70. Pajamas, dress, at Paraphernalia, 795 Madison Avenue, New York 10021

OPPOSITE PHOTOGRAPHED IN LON

In 1967, Rhodes and Ayton took a tiny two-room studio at the junction of Monmouth Street and Shaftesbury Avenue in Covent Garden across the street from their friend, model and textile designer Jacqui McLennan, who lived at 82 Neal Street. McLennan was able to see into their windows and was frequently called upon when Rhodes and Ayton needed to fit their newest creation, or model their latest collection when a buyer would suddenly call in. Rhodes and Ayton once rang in a panic asking if she would quickly wash and style her hair, throw some makeup and false eye lashes on as Molly Parkin from *Nova* was visiting the studio. Parkin's visit landed them in *Nova* in April 1967 under the headline

'Everything is coming up Pow. Painted patterns everywhere,'

providing the duo with their first piece of press featuring a dress in Rhodes's *Lightbulb* print.[48]

McLennan was frequently taken around London modelling Rhodes and Ayton's designs in exchange for the photographs for her portfolio. A chic model with her blond bob and exaggerated features, she suited the clothes perfectly and struck the attitude they were looking for. In one photo shoot in early 1967 McLennan stands in a rundown doorway in the old Covent Garden flower market modelling ensembles that used Rhodes's series of *Brick* prints on the exaggerated pockets of jackets, skirts, and dresses. The designs, given names such as *Candy*, *Kitty Fisher*, and *Mr Man*, were priced from £3 for a blouse to £10 for a coat. All outfits were offered in turquoise, pink, brown, or black. They travelled around London in McIntyre's car – the fashionable Mini – in which McLennan changed her outfits and they hopped out when they found a background that fitted their needs. On one early morning drive, they parked in Notting Hill and McLennan was photographed by another RCA graduate Roy Giles wearing a fitted black coat with a punchy *Mr Man and Lightbulb* printed waistcoat in front of a large graphic billboard of the Christian evangelist Billy Graham. These previously unpublished images demonstrate the spirit of collaboration and creativity in the '60s and how friends and partners were working together to break new ground. It typified the youth ethos of the 1960s that 'Anything was possible'.

The Fulham Road Clothes Shop came to fruition as Rhodes and Ayton wanted to increase their market not solely relying on their wholesale business, (which would fuel the boutique) as there were so few multi brand

retail outlets for the young and vibrant designs they were producing. Buyers were keen on Rhodes and Ayton's silhouettes though they were worried about the prints, the prevailing fashion for the mass market had been based around a fashionable colour and style of garment, which everyone would wear. Following in the footsteps of Mary Quant, Foale and Tuffin, Kiki Byrne, James Wedge and others they decided to open a boutique.

Rhodes and Ayton along with two other partners, Annette Green and Adrian Hughes, joined forces in 1968 to open the Fulham Road Clothes Shop at 160 Fulham Road in Chelsea. The shop was close to the King's Road, the epicentre of Swinging London in the late 1950s and early 1960s where the Chelsea Set hung out in boutiques like Bazaar and Top Gear as well as the new coffee shops. Fulham Road was beginning to become fashionable when Rhodes and Ayton began their venture; *Drapers Record* noted in 1968

'As rumour has it, the King's Road is on the wane, the Fulham Road, merely a stone's throw away, is very much alive'.[49]

Annette Green, a professional photographer, had been instrumental in finding an investor for the enterprise. Green convinced the British actress Vanessa Redgrave, whom she had been photographing, that their new boutique was worth the financial risk. The partners approached Redgrave with their ideas and she agreed to invest £1,000.[50] The four partners combined their money and the Fulham Road Clothes Shop was born. With the new shop venture, it was agreed that Rhodes would design half of the clothing along with the textiles; Ayton then began to show Rhodes how to make dress patterns and grade them. Green was in charge of the publicity photographs and Adrian Hughes acted as the shop manager. Adrian George, a graphic designer (also an RCA graduate) was hired to create the Fulham Road Clothes Shop logo loosely based around the brand identity on the packaging of frozen chunky chips. Interior design was also crucially important to the boutique and they pushed the conventions of shop displays, including an avant garde window display designed by a group called "Moonlight and Sun". The *Sunday Times* in 1968 described the innovative window:

'Four squares of strip neon, one set inside the other, wink, flash, and flicker from a silver-reflecting window. The colours and the speed change according to the volume and pitch of the traffic outside.'[51]

The flashing neon lights attracted passersby who then had to go downstairs to enter the boutique. The interior of the shop created by

Opposite Zandra Rhodes and Sylvia Ayton wearing brick print motif mini dresses with model in their beloved *Sequin Bikini* print, circa 1967.

Above Sylvia Ayton and Zandra Rhodes's *Lightbulbs* print dress in *Nova*, April 1967.

[48] *Nova*, April 1967.

[49] *Drapers Record*, 27 July 1968.

[50] Sylvia Ayton, interview with author, 3 December 2009.

[51] *Sunday Times*, 16 June 1968.

Jacqui McLennan modelling
Sylvia Ayton and Zandra
Rhodes's collection around
London, 1966. McLennan was
a fellow textile student at the
RCA with Rhodes, where they
formed a fast friendship. In
Covent Garden Rhodes and
Ayton had their studio across
from McLennan's flat, she
frequently modelled the
duo's designs for buyers and
fashion editors. Courtesy of
Roy A. Giles.

Left Zandra Rhodes reclining in the Fulham Road Clothes Shop wearing Lipstick print trousers in a solemn moment, 1968. This rare photograph shows the unique spacious decor of the shop – the two levels, white walls with photographs of Rhodes and Ayton's newest looks, and clothes organised for ease of browsing.

Below left Fulham Road Clothes Shop Catalogue, 1968. Courtesy of Sylvia Ayton

Opposite Fulham Road Clothes Shop poster on shiny ridged reflective 3D paper, number 87 out of an edition of 100. Designed by Adrian George 1968.

52 Vogue, June 1968.

53 Vamping It Up press clipping from Zandra Rhodes Archive, Press Book 1967-1968.

54 1 guinea = 21 shillings, 20 shillings = 1 pound.

55 Evening Post, 7 October 1968.

56 Evening Post, 7 October 1968.

57 Dierdre Mcsharry, 'A Touch of Lipstick on Satin', Daily Express, 1968, Zandra Rhodes Archive. Press Book 1967-1968.

58 Drapers Record 27 July 1968.

Alex McIntyre and Neville Green reflected the vogue for modernist décor in boutiques. The Fulham Road Clothes Shop had 'all white walls with photographs of their current designs taken by Annette Green blown-up giant sized.'[52]

'The wide foyer in the shop gives a feeling of unlimited space, such is the pleasureable change from most boutiques where moving from one rack to another is like walking in a maze. Mirrored pillars disguise the changing cubicles, satinised aluminum abounds, and illuminated fibreglass clothes racks are in keeping with the white interior. Coloured slides of all the garments in the shop are projected onto one wall and change every 3 seconds.'[53]

Customers could then see how the outfits would appear on the body and how they could be styled. The shop had specially designed rubber furniture and hand-printed Mellinex mirrors, all adding to a perfectly curated environment. For the opening of the shop in June 1968, Joe Cocker played to hundreds attending the event.

The Fulham Road Clothes Shop was open every day from 10:30am to 8pm and on Friday evenings to 9pm. Prices for the clothes in the boutique ranged from £3 for a silk printed scarf to 13 guineas for a two-tone jersey wool suit and 11 guineas for a heavy satin printed tunic with plain trousers.[54] Rhodes and Ayton tried to produce two new styles every week to refresh the selection in the shop; a high turnover rate of new styles in the boutique kept customers returning and was a key point of difference from the large department stores, which had a slower turnover of goods. They could also react faster to trends and respond to best selling items. The boutique was not geared towards a particular age. Rhodes and Ayton told the Evening Post,

"We don't design for an age bracket. We design for a type. Working girls want easy clothes for day and mad party gear. Anyone can wear our clothes if they're young at heart."[55]

Praise for the duo's designs soon poured in:
'Sylvia and Zandra are unique in that they do all their own fabric print designs as well as designing the clothes themselves. They've done some pretty exciting things with prints... Their use of prints hit the fashion headlines when they produced a printed suede suit, the print featured neon flowers and was confined to the full sleeves of the beige suede twosome.'[56]

Fashion reporter Deidre Mcsharry in 1968 wrote, 'You can tell a Fulham Road Dress at 40 paces back by the prints.'[57] Drapers Record noted the importance of the 'bold chintzy prints and highly contemporary styles',[58]

featured in the shop whilst *Women's Wear Daily* commented on the way 'prints and plains [are] put together in witty ways...the prints are many coloured abstracts splashed against plains as puff sleeves, pockets or edgings on dresses, coats and trousers.'[59]

The clothes they were printing, designing, and producing were garnering media attention, especially Rhodes's revolutionary textile designs. The prints evoked a youthfulness that reflected the dominant sensibility of sixties popular culture but also reflected the Pop Art idea of ugly as beautiful. Rhodes consciously worked with crude, disquieting colours and ideas in order to produce something new. *Women's Wear Daily* reported in August 1969:

'She turns what most people think of as vulgar into a new kind of art. Like the lipsticks she sent slithering across pale blue satin...the teddy bears that danced across canvas and suede.'[60]

Rhodes's textiles developed over a period of time drawing on themes and motifs of past designs, the prints becoming more figurative overall. Textiles created for the collections at the Fulham Road Clothes Shop were inspired by advertising, the popular low art beloved by the Pop Artists. The famous and much copied *Lipstick* print has its origins in a beauty

advertisement for Christian Dior's 'les sables pastels' photographed by Guy Bourdin. It featured a profile of a woman's face placed horizontally on the page with three fingers of each hand lined up next to each other. Rhodes pasted the advert on to her studio wall and reinterpreted the shape of the fingers as lipsticks, and by extension began to sketch lipsticks along with lips in her sketchbooks and into more formalised textile designs. *Lipstick* print was used for trousers, skirts, dresses, and blouses with the duo commenting, "People like to write with lipstick. Our prints do it for them."[61] This witty comment exemplifies Rhodes and Ayton's irreverent attitude towards dressing. The same Dior advertisement shot by Bourdin was also the starting point for the print *Hands and Flowers*, which featured hands with polished nails holding a large flower, or bouquet of flowers in a vertical design used on blouses and in billowy cape type sleeves.

Rhodes revisited earlier motifs such as her series of *Lightbulb* prints, which she and Ayton made into a fashionable paper dress in punchy colours of florescent pink and yellow on white ground. Paper dresses at the time were

Right Long printed scarf by Sylvia Ayton and Zandra Rhodes, Fulham Road Clothes Shop.

Opposite Lightbulb paper dress featured in *Nova*, Sylvia Ayton and Zandra Rhodes, 1968, Harri Peccinotti.

[59] *Women's Wear Daily*, 14 December 1966.

[60] *Women's Wear Daily*, 27 August 1969.

[61] Deirdre Mcsharry, 'A Touch of Lipstick on Satin', *Daily Express*, 1968, Zandra Rhodes Archive Press Book 1967-1968.

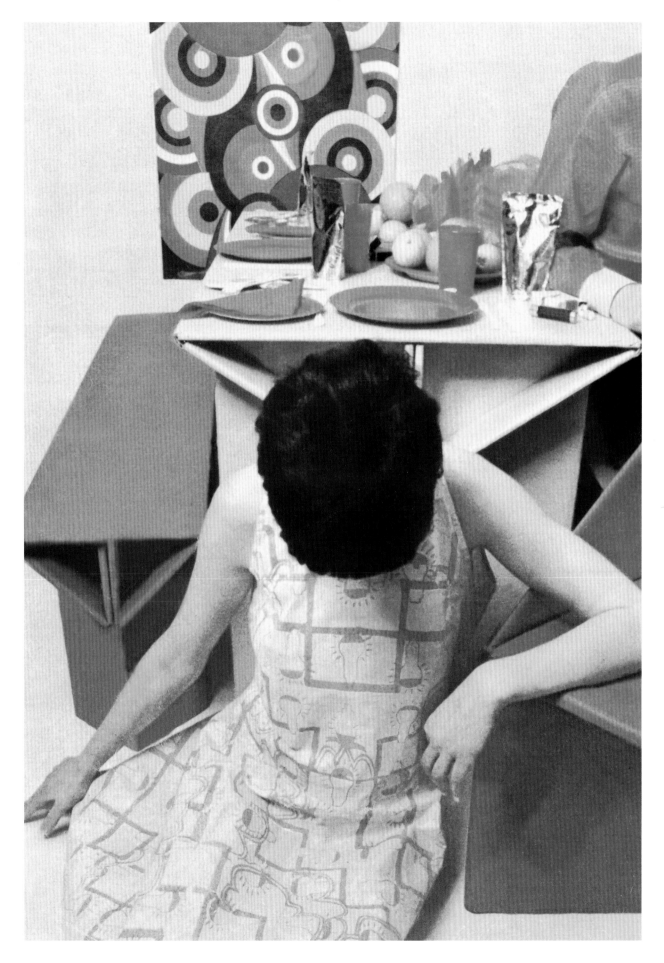

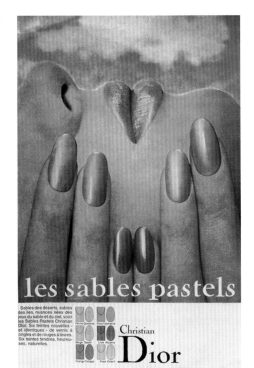

les sables pastels

Christian Dior

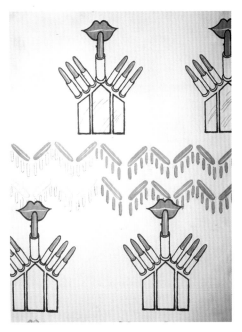

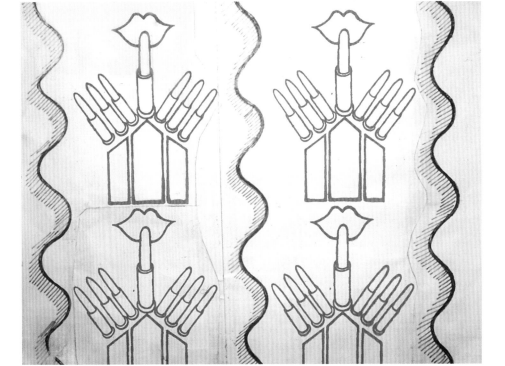

Opposite Lipstick print mini skirt by Sylvia Ayton and Zanda Rhodes featured in *Vogue* April 1968. Stephen Bobroff/Vogue ©The Condé Nast Publications Ltd.

Above Christian Dior beauty advertisement, which influenced Rhodes's *Hands and Flowers* and *Lipstick* prints. Courtesy of Guy Bourdin.

Top left Lipstick and lips ideas from Rhodes's sketchbook.

Top right Lipstick paper design with neon motifs creeping into the design.

Bottom right Lipstick paper design with wiggle.

the height of throwaway fashion and the paper medium took bold prints well, creating statement garments. Rhodes and Ayton were amongst the first on the bandwagon. The

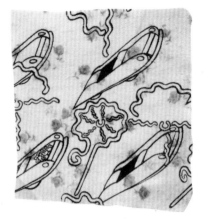

Lightbulb paper dress was a commercial success for them, though the Miss Selfridge buyer did ring the design duo wondering how to get the shop's customers from incredulously tearing the hems of the dresses to see if it really was paper.[62] Rhodes also used her earlier RCA designs for neon lights transforming them into *Neon Flowers and Grid*, with neon tube lighting in wiggly flower-like shapes juxtaposed on a ridged grid pattern printed on felt. The neons and comic motifs were meshed together to form the *Neon and Comics* prints where Rhodes added a version of Lady Penelope's FAB 1 Rolls Royce from her favourite television programme *Thunderbirds*. Rhodes and Ayton took the Neon print series one-step further repackaging them into body transfers exclusive to the Harrods Way In department in the summer of 1968, where the duo gave demonstrations on models. The *Evening Post* noted,

'Sylvia and Zandra are sold on the idea of powerful prints, which they like to back up with body transfers and tattoo patterns.'[63]

The *Daily Express* headline ran 'For Summer Nuttiness – the Instant Tattoo…transfers for big girls are more like avant garde tattoos. They are bracelets and belt shapes, men in gangster hats, sports cars, abstract flowers and a few odd squiggles and lines.'[64] The transfers were a subcultural and unconventional statement, irreverent without being dangerous. They also showed how Rhodes and Ayton were open to permutations and commercial possibilities of the print.

The *Teddy Bear* print, which was printed on canvas and used in voluminous sleeves on blouses as well as an all-over print, took the neon tubes as its starting point using them in a diamond shape to separate the two rows of teddy bears. Rhodes then looked at the work of Parisian fashion designer Paco Rabanne with his sequin dresses and jewellery made of phosphorescent Rhodoid plastic discs strung with fine wire. She used this influence to design a range of sequin themed prints, reinterpreting Rabanne's innovative plastic dresses into a poppy colourful faux sequin print. In one incarnation, Rhodes arranged the print in the shape of a bikini, which was printed onto a white moiré tailored mini dress, a favourite design of both Rhodes and Ayton. The faux

Top *Lady Penelope Car and Neon Flower design*, one-colour print on floral flannelette, 1968.

Right Teddy Bear Sleeves – *Teddy Bear* sleeved printed blouse, Sylvia Ayton and Zandra Rhodes, 1968.

Opposite page Sylvia Ayton and Zandra Rhodes *Teddy Bear* sleeve blouse featured in *Nova*.

[62] Sylvia Ayton quoted in Fogg, p. 53.

[63] *Evening Post*, 7 Oct 1968.

[64] *Daily Express*, 1 July 1968.

bikini being an ironic play on the weather in England.

In June 1968, the *Sunday Times* commented: 'The prints themselves are totally new and different, striking but not harsh. Curving lines, dotted lines like stitching, writing signed with a lipstick case… are used on chiffon, crepe, cotton, satin and organdie.'[65] As a tribute to their backer, Rhodes designed a print for Vanessa Redgrave, entitled *We Love You Vanessa*, which was Rhodes's first experiment with incorporating handwritten words into the textile print. Throughout her school years, Rhodes had

'loved the way words look[ed], graphically' and she became passionate about calligraphy. [66]

This early fascination combined with her interest at the RCA in Jasper Johns's use of words and text in his artwork became a significant influence. Johns looked to ordinary objects from daily life such as flags and targets and used letters, numbers, and text throughout his work. From this example, Rhodes mirrored events happening in her own life onto her designs. Beginning with the Redgrave print, little poems, words, or thoughts crept into her prints becoming motifs in their own right. The *We Love You Vanessa* print was made into blouses and dresses. The handwritten words in the print contributed to its success and Rhodes developed this theme further in her textiles from the early 1970s onwards.[67]

Rhodes regarded her prints as having strong personalities of their own and she craved the freedom to explore the silhouettes based on the print, not the other way around. She also increasingly played with her appearance; designing herself as she would her textiles and this aspect of her self-expression blossomed but became problematic for Rhodes and Ayton's business. Rhodes wore very short skirts to the point where one could almost see her knickers and applied heavy colourful makeup, and wore two pairs of false eyelashes on each eye. She shaved back her hairline and wore a turban. Rhodes notes that her appearance even in those days was shocking whilst Ayton sometimes felt that Rhodes's appearance was hindering the saleability of their work. The strain of their working relationship was indicative of some of these issues. Sensing Rhodes's look was too extreme, Ayton would ask Rhodes to stay at the back of the shop so she would not scare the customers and fashion buyers away. Rhodes's appearance aside, there were larger financial issues that contributed to the failure of her partnership with Ayton and the Fulham Road Clothes Shop. Ayton says:

Right Fashion sketch by Sylvia Ayton of Rhodes's *Sequin* print inspired by Paco Rabanne, 1967. Courtesy of Sylvia Ayton.

Opposite, left Sequin Dress, Sylvia Ayton and Zandra Rhodes, 1966 Ronald Traeger/ Vogue ©The Condé Nast Publications Ltd.

Opposite, right Sequin paper artwork made up into Ayton's fashion sketch and photographed by *Vogue* in 1966.

[65] *Sunday Times*, 16 June 1968.

[66] Rhodes, p.10.

[67] Handwritten words appear again in the *Lovely Lilies* collection of textiles in 1972, specifically in *A Field of Lilies*, where Rhodes wrote in the print 'a field of lilies' and 'a field of lilies lots and lots of beautiful lilies a field of lilies and yet more lilies lots and lots of lilies. 'The *Reverse Lily* and *Lace Mountain* print also has 'lilies' written in the design of the print.

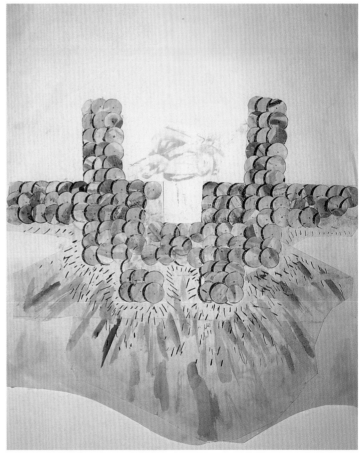

"We were not very good at [the business side of the enterprise], we liked designing and drawing too much. People owed us lots of money and we owed people lots of money. The bailiffs came quite often. It was frightening… I would hide in the bathroom until they had gone. We had no business sense and no financial sense, I don't even think we took a salary from the company. We had lots of publicity, but that doesn't always mean much in terms of sales. It was very sad."[68]

The shop folded a year after it had opened due to financial problems and the partners went their separate ways. Ayton went on to became an award-winning designer for Wallis, creating jackets and tailored clothes worn and loved by thousands.[69]

What Rhodes and Ayton took from the Fulham Road Clothes Shop was an audience who already existed but had not fully matured for their brightly printed clothes. Many friends told Rhodes she should not have opened the boutique without the proper financial details in place to make it viable, but in retrospect she is glad of the experience. "The very things we were told were the least commercial like the printed chiffon kaftans and the handkerchief point tiered trousers were what our shop sold best," she told *Women's Wear Daily* in 1969.[70] The experience of the Fulham Road Clothes Shop and the success of her printed silk chiffon scarves that she was selling from 1968 in America as a sideline venture, proved to Rhodes that she could survive as a young independent designer herself. She decided to branch out on her own, using her prints as she had always intended, dressing herself up how she pleased. All that was required was for Rhodes to advance her pattern making skills.

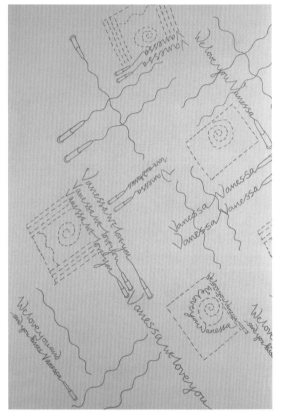

Top Zandra Rhodes in New York wearing the *Knitted Landscape* print scarf tied tightly around her head and trademark blue eye shadow, 1969, Ron Bowen.

Top right *Wiggle Square* print in a tiered top and trousers with matching scarf, Fulham Road Clothes Shop. Priced at 11 guineas, the ensemble was featured in *Vogue* June 1968. Arnaud de Rosnay/Vogue ©The Condé Nast Publications Ltd.

Bottom right *Vanessa We Love You (and send you kisses)*, one colour print on yellow rayon satin, 1967, Fulham Road Clothes Shop. Designed in honour of the shop's investor, Vanessa Redgrave, the print features Zandra Rhodes's first use of handwriting and the lipstick motif, which Rhodes developed further in prints for the label and boutique.

Opposite, top Knitted chain stitch ideas in Zandra Rhodes's sketchbook, circa 1968-9.

Opposite, bottom Circular knitted chain stitch sketches, circa 1968-9.

[68] Sylvia Ayton quoted in Fogg, p.53.

[69] Sylvia Ayton, interview with author, 3 December 2009.

[70] *Women's Wear Daily*, 27 August 1969.

[71] Zandra Rhodes, interview with author, 21 November 2009.

[72] Rhodes, p.26.

[73] Rhodes, p.26.

Next page, left Twins Oxana and Myroslava Prystay photograhed by David Bailey for British *Vogue* December 1969. They wear a dress and kaftan from the *Knitted Circle* collection composed of *Knitted Circle* and *Diamond and Roses* print, hand screen printed onto silk chiffon. Photo: Vogue/David Bailey ©The Condé Nast Publications Ltd.

Next page, right Yellow circular felt coats from *Knitted Circle* collection. The coat combines *Diamonds and Roses* and *Knitted Circle* prints. The main body of the coat with *Diamond and Roses* print consists of one large circle and the collar has cords and wooden beads attached to it. *Vogue* December 1969. Photo: Vogue/David Bailey ©The Condé Nast Publications Ltd.

Zandra Rhodes was now in a place where she could create the prints and clothes she dreamt of. Her first taste of success with her solo eponymous line was with long printed silk chiffon scarves that sold at boutiques and department stores in America with the assistance of her friend Richard Holley. She had met Holley at a party through Moya Bowler, a fellow RCA graduate and a famous shoe designer in the '60s and '70s.[71] Holley, a graduate from the prestigious Pratt Institute in New York, recognised that Rhodes's scarves would sell well in New York at high end shops and set out to sell her work. Their popularity was such that Richard Avedon used one of the silk chiffon scarves to cover the face of a model for a photo shoot in the October 1969 issue of American *Vogue*.

Nonetheless, Rhodes met with many prejudices as a trained textile designer who endeavored to design clothes. She was undeterred. The responses to the news that she would start her own line were met with scepticisim. Rhodes was told,

"Once a textile designer, always a textile designer," and that "a career cannot be changed mid-stream".[72]

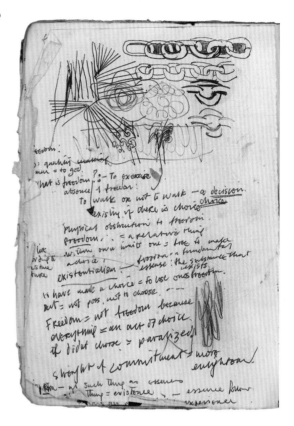

She turned to two friends who were at the RCA with her, Norman Baines and Leslie Poole, to teach her how to create dress patterns. They taught her how to make a paper pattern, about the grain of the fabric, and how to lay the pattern out amongst other technicalities. The most useful method they bestowed upon Rhodes was how to use her own body in the draping of the material, as she had done herself with her paper textiles panels where she would cut a hole out for her head.

"For the first time, I was experimenting with my own printed fabric, draping pieces over myself, walking around and moving the patterns and the colours. It was exhilarating", says Rhodes.[73]

This breakthrough prompted Rhodes to hire a machinist in 1969 and together they made Rhodes's first line of dresses, kaftans, and exotic felt coats the way she intended, without any compromises. She funded the venture herself with her earnings from teaching and the print studio.

Rhodes focused on the prints enhancing the garment instead of being overlooked in favour of the garment silhouette. In this way, Rhodes allowed the print to lead her to the shape of the garment, a novel idea in the late '60s. The usual practice was for designers to commission work or buy direct from textile

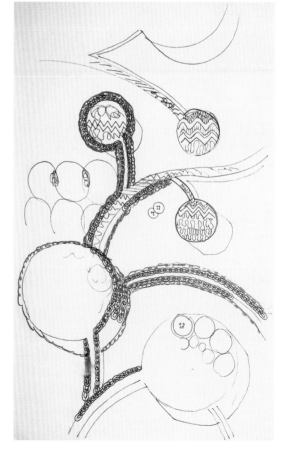

manufacturers; they would then cut into the print as they pleased to create their garments. Rhodes's singular approach meant that the fabric guided the design of both the textiles and the clothes. Her first solo collection, *Knitted Circle*, developed from this practice, and Rhodes let her creativity loose on her prints, clothes, and as ever, on her appearance.

The *Knitted Circle* collection comprised four prints, *Knitted Landscape Scarf*, *Knitted Circle*, *Wiggle Square* and *Diamonds and Roses*, the latter two prints and their motifs had been developed at the RCA and the Fulham Road Clothes Shop. *Knitted Circle* and *Knitted Landscape Scarf*, on the other hand, played with a new visual language and demonstrated a new maturity and intricacy to Rhodes's designs. The *Knitted Circle* print was influenced by holidays that Rhodes and MacIntyre would take to Wales with their close friends Janet Street-Porter, then fashion editor of *Petticoat*, and her husband Tim Street-Porter, a photographer. There, they took walks while bundled in knitted scarves, gloves, and hats; at night Rhodes and Street-Porter would knit by the fire; taking part in the beloved craft practice of hand knitting, a particularly British pastime with its cozy familiarity and room for individualism. Knitted chain stitches began to appear in Rhodes's sketchbook leading Rhodes to the Victoria and Albert Museum's textile study room, where she studied knitted bedspreads and embroidered bed hangings worked with wool yarns in chain stitches.

A fascination with the stitches themselves, how to reinterpret them flat but also how to form patterns with the chain stitch and colour combinations so they appeared to have a connection with knitting became a challenge within the design. Speaking to *Women's Wear Daily* in 1969, Rhodes noted that in producing the collection she

'wanted a print that had the feel of the knit, but couldn't possibly be knitted.'[74]

The large, printed cable stitches and cable stitch flowers of *Knitted Circle* have an inherent energy, a crafted dynamism that makes them feel as if someone picked up knitting needles and knitted them. However, Rhodes subverts the idea of handwork by creating an illusion of a printed knit on flat fabric with mechanically reproduced stitches. Rhodes incorporated vibrant primary colours of red, blue, and yellow into the print giving it a Pop edge.

In the *Knitted Circle* collection of prints, Rhodes's signature wiggles appear for the first time and start to take a central part of her textiles. Initially wiggles were incorporated with the *Wiggle Square* print from 1968, as a

[74] *Women's Wear Daily*, 27 August 1969.

[75] Rhodes, p. 10.

[76] Rhodes, p. 26.

[77] *Harpers Bazaar* (British), April 1970.

secondary feature. The wiggles gained a wider prominence in the prints, emerging as fillers between the larger knitted circle motifs as well as little mountain-like shapes bordering the inside of the circle, drawing the eye towards the knitted flowers and circular chains. The emergence of the wiggles is another example of a recurring motif derived from the designer's past. She has suggested that the fret shapes of the jigsaw puzzles that she played with on holiday as young girl 'must have been the first wiggles to become imprinted in her mind's eye.'[75] A part of Rhodes's design vernacular, the wiggles appear in most of the prints either taking the form of a central motif, as an element to fill background space, or as a shape within a larger design.

As the *Knitted Circle* print was designed in circles, Rhodes cut around these to produce the shape of her garments.

'I had designed in a circle. Now I cut in circles, sewed in circles, and at last, the creative circle was complete. I made swirling, dramatic shapes with no concessions to the saleable, the acceptable, or the ordinary. The true Rhodes style came into being.'[76]

Continuing her method of print dictating silhouette, she produced modern whimsical shapes printed on the finest silk chiffon, heavy felt, quilted satin and lurex, which stood out from those of other contemporary designers. *Harper's Bazaar* observed,

'She uses rich, striking fabrics, silk chiffon, quilted satin, printed felt, and her designs are wide, expansive, extravagant. "Dream clothes, I call them" Rhodes says. And this is their appeal for people like Britt Eckland, who loves to wear them and actress Edina Ronay'.[77]

The *Knitted Circle* collection comprised fifteen garments and was presented to London fashion editors, a few buyers at speciality department stores as well as in New York late in 1969. Richard Holley insisted that Rhodes accompany him on a trip back to New York where she could be introduced to the fashion scene and start making her mark on America. The editor of English *Vogue*, Beatrix Miller, introduced her to Diana Vreeland, then the editor-in-chief of American *Vogue*, and to June Weir, chief editor of *Women's Wear Daily*. Through these contacts, the New York fashion world opened up to her: Rhodes's designs were photographed for a full fashion story in *Vogue* modelled by actress Natalie Wood, *Women's Wear Daily* ran a feature on her and other revered fashion magazines followed suit. Geraldine Stutz, then esteemed President of the exclusive high-end New York department store Henri Bendel, bought Rhodes's entire collection and placed the dresses, kaftans, and coats front and centre of their window displays. Stutz commented:

'I feel differently about Zandra than I do other designers…She's not a professional designer but rather an artist who has chosen clothes as a medium. Her clothes are glorious fantasies. They have everything to do with style and nothing to do with fashion. They are timeless, spectacular, wonderful to wear and marvelous to look at.'[78]

Glittering society ladies of the New York set such as such as Evangeline Bruce (wife of the US ambassador to the UK), Chessy Rayner, and Mica Ertegün, snapped up Rhodes's collection. This breakthrough for a high-end clientele who established the tone for fashion and interior decoration proved Rhodes's designs were commercial enough to compete in the tough New York fashion market. It also showed that Rhodes's work had a wider and more varied audience than the Swinging London youth culture and thrived in a different context. Chic boutiques and stores such as Marshall Fields, I. Magnin & Co, and Marthas and Sakowitz also bought the *Knitted Circle* collection in 1969-70 adding to Rhodes's growing list of stockists in America.

The fashion press were in awe of Rhodes's complete vision. American *Vogue* commented:

'Zandra Rhodes, [is] a young London designer who makes the hand-printed fabrics as well as the clothes themselves. There are things you could wear anywhere, anytime – like the circle of chrome-yellow felt, swirling with scarlet patterns; you could wear it as a coat, a robe, a dress, anything you like…imagine how delicious it would look billowing out behind you as you drift down some great flight of stairs.'[79]

The June 1970 issue of American *Vogue* featured the silk chiffon dresses, skirts, and blouses in the *Knitted Circle* collection in a spread entitled 'Mid Summer Light Dreams' photographed by Irving Penn. 'Zandra Rhodes' hand printed chiffon designs are fantasy things that flutter and blow and wrap you in color mixed of light, dreams, air.'[80] Rhodes's use of silk chiffon, which lent itself beautifully to colour when printed and moved gracefully with the body, contributed to the fantasy element that *Vogue* described. The fashion editorials used a descriptive form of language to describe abstract notions in fine art such as light, dreams, and air. These comparisons continued, using specific artists' names, 'Yards and yards of purest fantasy – The cloud of pink and blue is like an enchanted figure floating across a Chagall sky' and 'fascinating, like a Magritte painting,'[81] highlighting the inspiration behind and the artistry and painterly qualities with which she designed her prints and garments.

Upon Rhodes's return to London from her trip, she did not have a retail outlet for her collection. Beatrix Miller of *Vogue* and her fashionable swinging editress of the 'Young

Ideas' section, Marit Allen, introduced Rhodes to Anne Knight, Merchandise Director of Fortnum and Mason, the up-market department store in Piccadilly. Knight, who was promoting young British fashion designers in the Odyssey Room, billed as 'the great new fashion adventure', bought Rhodes's collection along with designs from Bill Gibb and Jean Muir.[82] 'There, at imagination's edge find a trio of unique designers…Their views, alien to everything mundane. Their clothes, un-alike and unlike any others.'[83] British *Vogue* took the lead of American *Vogue*, supporting Rhodes editorially through the magazine including a long quilted satin dress as well as the short version of the same design in a feature spread photographed by Clive Arrowsmith.

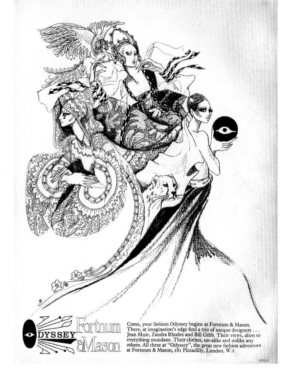

Come, your fashion Odyssey begins at Fortnum & Mason. There, at imagination's edge find a trio of unique designers . . . Jean Muir, Zandra Rhodes and Bill Gibb. Their views, alien to everything mundane. Their clothes, un-alike and unlike any others. All three at "Odyssey", the great new fashion adventure at Fortnum & Mason, 181 Piccadilly, London, W.1

Right Fortnum and Mason Odyssey Room advertisement featuring Zandra Rhodes, Bill Gibb and Jean Muir. Courtesy of Library, Central Saint Martin's.

Opposite *Knitted Circle* quilted satin dress featured in *Vogue* January 1970. Clive Arrowsmith/Vogue ©The Condé Nast Publications Ltd.

[78] Julie Kavanagh, 'How London's Eccentric Fashion Designer Creates Her Glorious Fantasies', *W Magazine*, 23 January 1976.

[79] *Vogue* (American), January 1970.

[80] *Vogue* (American), June 1970.

[81] *Vogue* (American), January 1970 and Milbank, p.114.

[82] Rhodes's collections retailed between £65 and £150 at Fortnum and Mason between 1969 and 1971.

[83] Fortnum and Mason Odyssey Room advertisement

Zandra Rhodes' parrot fashion,

Rhodes's appearance continued to evolve as her textile and fashions designs did. She wore her own flamboyant clothes with rainbow-coloured make-up, plucked eyebrows and eccentric hairstyles and hair colours, creating an extraordinary persona for herself. This persona would prove to be an extension of her creativity – as a textile designer she viewed everything as a surface to decorate. A pronounced interest in make-up, relating to her mother's exotic appearance and tutor Barbara Brown's style, were key factors in the creation of Rhodes's appearance and why she began to experiment with her face. Rhodes remarking, "I was always playing with make-up."[84]

'This "face" represents many things to [a woman]. It is at once a mask to shrink behind in a way of flaunting herself and exaggerating life. It is something separate, to be assembled and donned at will, and yet it becomes as much her own as her flesh and bones.'[85]

Rhodes's painted "face" would become as much a part of her image and the expression of her identity as her textile designs.

"As an extension of this type of designing, I used myself as a canvas with no compromise, experimenting with my image, using cosmetics, and my hair to create an impact."[86]

She would forever look apart from her peers and garner attention for it.

However, notoriety was a double-edged sword. While Rhodes was expressing her freedom through appearance, she was also masking her lack of confidence. Rhodes has described herself as insecure and introverted, and these traits have played a large part in the development of her appearance; insecurities are the very stuff of makeup.[87] For instance, Rhodes used the same bright blue colour as those in the *Sparkle* print from 1970-71, rubbing huge circles of blue eye shadow around her eyes and

wearing different colors of lipstick on each lip. Her appearance worked in a contradictory way: it called attention to her, attracting certain types, yet worked to intimidate, protecting her from her own vulnerability. By using herself as a canvas and making herself up in bold colours, similar to the colours she was using in her textiles, Rhodes could communicate to others without having to put herself on the line. Rhodes believed that if she does not look like anybody else she could not be compared to anyone and, by extension, her work would also be

exempt from comparison. Rhodes realized early on from her first experiments in the world of textile design that she was singular and fitted into nobody else's shoes. This meant Rhodes was the best promoter and advertisement of her clothes, she represented the whole, not just a facet. This drove Rhodes to the conclusion that only she could 'model' and represent her own prints and clothes – her brand.

With the creation of her eponymous line 'Zandra Rhodes', Rhodes began to unify her appearance, knitting together the inspirations she used for her prints, her fashion designs and then applying them to her outward appearance – Rhodes's vision was now complete. She took her already provocative look and merged it with her designs. She wore her printed *Knitted Landscape* scarf and other prints wrapped tightly around her head and used dramatic and colourful eyeshadow. Joan Juliet Buck, then a young writer and girl about town, remembers how Rhodes used Pentel felt tip pens as eyeliner.[88] She also drew artificial curls onto her forehead and cheeks with eyebrow pencils and lipstick. Rhodes recreated this dramatic look for the cover of *Queen* styling the model to replicate her own look. Rhodes was an amalgamation of print from head to toe, a self-created sort of an artistic Warholian Pop persona. The *Vogue* editor was directly inspired by Rhodes's original image and instructed hair stylist Franklyn Welsh to use Rhodes's hairstyle for the models in the 'Mid Summer Light Dreams'

Far left Zandra Rhodes wearing *Bricks* print mini dress, Fulham Road Clothes Shop, 1968. Courtesy of Steve Hyatt.

Left and below Zandra Rhodes in *Chevron Shawl* kaftan at home. These two images were featured in Australian *Women's Weekly* on 30 June, 1971 to promote her Sekers Australia fabrics. Courtesy of Alec Murray.

[84] Zandra Rhodes, interview with author, 21 November 2009

[85] Kennedy Fraser, *The Fashionable Mind*, New York, Alfred A. Knoff, 1981, p. 20.

[86] Zandra Rhodes, interview with author, 21 November 2009

[87] Zandra Rhodes, interview with author, 21 November 2009.

[88] Joan Juliet Buck, interview with author, 12 January 2010.

feature stating 'Coiffures on these four pages, sprigged with curls the way Zandra Rhodes does her own hair.'[89]

Hair was as equally important an aspect to Rhodes as make-up in her look. She wanted to achieve green hair in early 1970 and went directly to Vidal Sassoon who had cut her hair in the early sixties but he refused to dye it, as it was too dark and offered her a bright green wig instead, which made her head ache. Celebrity hairstylist Leonard was brave enough to dye her hair, Rhodes providing him with the exact dye that she used for printing textiles. This was also the beginning of a long and vibrant working relationship for Rhodes and Leonard who went on to create hairstyles for Rhodes's catwalk shows and collection posters. Whilst designing the *Chevron Shawl* collection of 1970, Rhodes sewed real feathers to the ends of her printed handkerchief pointed silk chiffon skirts and then extended this idea to herself, gluing feathers on the end of her hair with eyelash glue. Her styles changed constantly: once Rhodes created a rainbow effect with long multi-coloured tufts of hair. The *Sunday Times* in July 1971 stated:

'When I say Zandra Rhodes looks like nothing on earth, I mean it quite literally: she looks more like a tropical butterfly than a person. Her hair is dyed, in streaks – cerise, orange, blue and green – her cheeks and eyes are painted red, her forehead streaked with it and instead of eyebrows (hers have disappeared under white paint) she puts three sequins (sometimes green, sometimes cerise) where they would have started.'[90]

Her physical self, as a canvas and test palette, played a central role in the entire design process of Rhodes's creative output. Throughout the last forty years Rhodes has strived to create a complete image for herself and collections – textiles, clothes, make-up, hair, accessories, which she has extended to the models in her fashion shows with the assistance of other artists and designers such as Andrew Logan, Richard Sharah, Mick Milligan, Phyllis Cohen, Trevor Sorbie and Leonard.

Opposite Zandra Rhodes dramatically posed in Angelo Donghia's apartment on her second visit to New York. She wears her circular cape combining *Wiggle and Check*, in two colourways, and *Tasselled Circle* with feathers glued to the ends of her hair, 1970. Terrance McCarten

Above Zandra Rhodes in a more casual look wearing overalls with her silk chiffon knitted circle print blouse and chunky necklaces, 1971, Bishin Jumoniji.

[89] *Vogue* (American) 1970 June.

[90] *Sunday Times*, 25 July 1971.

Above Zandra Rhodes in the
Fulham Road Clothes Shop
with scarf tied around her
head decorated with brooches.

Opposite Cover of *Queen*,
Zandra Rhodes styled the model
and acted as the make-up artist
on this cover shoot, recreating
her own colourful dramatic
look, January 1969. Courtesy
of Tim Street-Porter.

queen

10th DEC - 6th JAN

CHRISTMAS SPECIAL 2. 5s

HIGH
HIGH
HIGH
HIGH GOTHIC
THE STYLE OF THE SEVENTIES

A model wearing Rhodes's
Chevron Shawl silk chiffon
kaftan, 1970. Bill Cunningham

Ernestine Carter in the *Sunday Times* vividly recalled entering Rhodes's design studio for the first time: 'In her Bayswater workrooms you can see the caterpillar and the cocoon. As you enter a blank blue door, great whiffs of paint prepare you for narrow stairs blocked with silk-screen frames, narrow passages full of buckets of paint, and, as you mount to the top, rolls of Zandra's fabrics. This journey through the studio is the logical progression as Zandra designs, makes the negatives and silk-screens, and prints her fabrics.'[91] Hand-printing and hand-making the resulting fashion collection was rare for a designer during this period, many of whom rejected couture methods, and relied upon fast manufacturing practices. During the golden age of couture from the late 1940s to the 1950s, such artisanal techniques were the norm for the industry that prided themselves on luxury, quality, and provenance. Rhodes was passionate that her collections of both textiles and the resulting garments were hand crafted and couture based. This marked a shift from her earlier thoughts on the production of the clothing, taking complete control of the entire design process enabled Rhodes to see the benefits.

Despite Rhodes's colourful and eccentric creations she complied with the fashion system of designing and presenting two collections a year, which straddled the boundaries of high-end ready-to-wear and *haute couture*. For lack of an appropriate title, her work was referred to as 'new couture'. Gillian Edwards reporting for the *Observer Review* stated:

'The British have always had a reputation abroad for excelling in eccentricity in dress; Zandra Rhodes leads it today with her otherworldly look and her far-outness…Visiting European fashion experts often ask if couture still exists in London. How extraordinary and unexpected to be able to reply "Yes, Zandra Rhodes is the new couture".'[92]

Her distinctive approach – the total control of all aspects of the design from printed textiles, to silhouettes, to accessories – gained Rhodes press attention. Rhodes's dresses 'certainly approach the craftsman and the prices – of the old couture' but as she says, "my dresses don't go according to the old idea of how a dress should be made."[93]

American fashion designer Bill Blass concurred, "She represents an original approach to clothes."[94]

Opposite Penelope Tree models kaftan style jacket in *Chevron Shawl* print on silk chiffon for Italian *Vogue*. The kaftan is cut to the shape of the print with feather trim. Zandra Rhodes incorporated the feathers to her look glueing them to the ends of her hair. Photo: Vogue/ David Bailey ©The Condé Nast Publications Ltd.

[91] *Sunday Times*, 25 July 1971.

[92] *Observer Review*, 25 June 1972.

[93] *Sunday Telegraph Magazine*, 10 December 1972.

[94] Bill Blass quoted in Julie Kavanagh, 'How London's Eccentric Fashion Designer Creates Her Glorious Fantasies', *W Magazine*, 30 January 1976.

TRIM "TRIPLE POWER FLOWER 65" & VICE VERSA HAND SCREEN PRINT DESIGN BY ZANDRA R...

Opposite *Diamond and Roses with Knitted Chains*, three-colour print on poly cotton, Zandra Rhodes for Mafia, 1970.

Above *Triple Flower Power 65*, Hand screen printed wallpaper, Zandra Rhodes for &Vice Versa, 1970.

With Rhodes's first collection a success
both commercially and editorially, special
commissions came pouring in. They all wanted
her innovative textile designs to adorn their
scarves, wallpapers, and fabrics, in motifs
and designs that were quickly becoming
recognizably Rhodes. Her first commission in

1970 was for Jacqmar
Fabrics Ltd, the English
purveyor of luxury silk
scarves. Jacqmar was
originally a supplier of
fine silks to the Paris
couture houses from
the mid-1930s onwards;
the directors saw there
was a profit to be
made with their offcuts
of fabric and created
a sideline silk scarf
business. Jacqmar was
known in the 1940s and
1950s for its printed
head squares with
creative propaganda
themes produced
during World War II and had retained its flair
for design in the '60s and '70s.

The commission came through Julius
Schofield who first met Rhodes in the mid-1960s
as the editor of fashion forecasting publication,
Trends. *Trends* was an industry magazine
looking at yarn, fibres, textiles, and fashion,
touring the dye factories, textile mills, art school
and diploma shows for new talent as well as
visiting studios. Schofield, along with Joanna
Neicho, founded Indesign, a recruitment agency
for fashion and textile design talent in 1968.
For Rhodes, Schofield secured the Jacqmar
commission, a series of scarves with three
designs hand-printed onto silk twill and silk
chiffon. The designs featured elements of *Snail
Flower* print, *Wiggle and Check*, her signature
wiggles, and wiggle tassels, which Rhodes
developed further in a set of textiles for her
Chevron Shawl collection of the same year.

On Rhodes's first trip to New York she was
introduced to Angelo Donghia, one of the top
interior designers in the States and a partner in
the firm Burge-Donghia Interiors. His interiors
were immediately identifiable with the
trademark silver foil ceilings, lacquered walls,
bleached floors, and generously upholstered
furniture that his society and celebrity clients
adored. In 1968 Donghia had begun to diversify
when the young designer Seymour Avigdor

Above *Snail Flower
and Wiggle* scarf,
three-colour print on
silk twill, Zandra Rhodes
for Jacqmar, 1970.

Opposite *Fringed
Shawl*, three-colour
print on poly cotton,
Zandra Rhodes for
Mafia, 1970.

[95] Zandra Rhodes,
interview with author,
20 March 2010.

[96] &Vice Versa Archive

[97] &Vice Versa Archive

[98] For further information
on Zandra Rhodes Living
collection with CVP please
see Dennis Nothdruft,
'Blurring the Boundaries:
Print, Personality and the
Interiors of Zandra Rhodes
and CVP' in *Decorative
Arts Society Journal*,
no 33, 2009, pp. 26–37.

[99] Sophie Chapdelaine de
Montvalon, *Le Beau Pour
Tous*, Paris, L'Iconoclaste,
2009, p. 214.

came to him with fabric designs. Recognizing that they would be successful, Donghia established a separate company called &Vice Versa to manufacture fabrics and wallcoverings from Avigdor and other young designers such as Rhodes. Rhodes remembers Donghia was taken with her bold colourful appearance on their introduction, telling her

'If you look like that then you must create wonderful work and I have to see it".[95]

The following day she brought designs to his studio; Donghia commissioned a line of hand-printed wallpapers and furnishing fabrics on the spot. The collection (six designs made into both wallpaper and furnishing fabric) was based on the Donghia's favourite textiles and certain motifs such as wiggles, wiggle tassels, flower-like shapes, snail flower and cut out circles.[96] Back in London, Rhodes created the collection for &Vice Versa in appealing colourways to suit varied tastes. The final product was hand screen printed wallpapers on

vinyl and metallic mylar like Donghia's signature ceilings and heavy cotton fabrics. Rhodes's wallpapers for &Vice Versa were priced between $13-14 per roll for the vinyl wallcovering, $20-22 per roll for the mylar wallcovering, and $11 – 12.50 a yard for the furnishing fabric.[97] They were given names that reflected '60s swinging London such as *Triple Flower Power 65*, to attract the trendy New York metropolitan market. This foray into interior design would be a precursor to Rhodes's own brand of home furnishing fabrics and wallpapers in collaboration with interior designer Christopher Vane Percy of CVP, Zandra Rhodes Living and their wholesale company By The Yard By The Yard.[98]

The final important commission of this time was with the pioneering Parisian design agency Mafia created by Maime Arnodin and Denise Fayolle who strove to eliminate ugliness in the world of design. Through the agency they assembled a team of specialists in graphic and industrial design, as well as publicity – offering a diverse range of services to their clients, aiming to strengthen their own brand and achieve control in all stages of consumer design. Mafia sought to discover and promote new ideas and talent outside France, and Rhodes's textiles fitted perfectly with their aim. Mafia handpicked Rhodes amongst other leading designers such as Kenzo, Claude Montana, Thierry Mugler, and Hanae Mori for fashion commissions.

Fashion photographer David Bailey initially introduced Rhodes to the pioneering duo in 1969; Rhodes consequently flew to Paris to discuss the commissioning of a textile and dress collection for Du Pont de Nemours, a client of Mafia, to promote their new fabrics.[99] As with Rhodes's earlier comissions, Arnodin and Fayolle chose specific themes from her portfolio of designs, diamond and roses, knitted chain stitching, wiggles, and wiggle tassels in a chevron pattern were to be included in the collection of textiles for Du Pont. The textiles were silkscreened onto polycotton and made into stylish garments. The commission secured by Mafia and the subsequent trips to Paris put Rhodes in contact with the leading lights of Parisian fashion and interior design, meeting amongst others Emmanuelle Kahn, Karl Lagerfeld, Sonia Rykiel, and Andrée Putman.

Many of the motifs in the textiles used for the Jacqmar, &Vice Versa, and Mafia commissions were extracted from Zandra Rhodes's second collection *Chevron Shawl*, composed of four elaborate textiles designs. For Rhodes, this collection combined traditional English Victoriana with the fashionable peasant look that was becoming increasingly popular in London and Paris. Sketches and doodles of Victorian fringed shawls made their way into her sketchbooks, drawing the fringe with wiggle tassel like forms next to simplified flowers in the centre of a triangular shawl; this became the *Chevron Shawl* print. Rhodes recalls heavily embroidered tasselled shawls were very popular in the early 1970s, with many friends wrapping them around their clothes or

even wearing the scarves as skirts with the tassels blowing freely. Other inspirations stemmed from the *Knitted Circle* collection of textiles, this time studying embroidery, which manifested itself throughout the print. Further developments from this original textile and its rough interpretations of embroidery stitches and pattern were *Wiggle and Check*, *Snail Flower*, a large stylized hollyhock flower with wiggles, and *Tasselled Circle*, which was designed purely as a circle with tassels without interlocking motifs like the *Knitted Circle* print.

This collection of textiles proved to work well on many fabrics allowing Rhodes room to experiment with different types: on stiff calico, a pointed dramatic quilted coat was designed following the shape of the pointed zigzag tassels in the *Chevron Shawl* print; the lightest silk chiffon was crafted into airy handkerchief-pointed hem skirts and dresses; and on quilted silk, voluminous Jacquard satin pleated dresses with a peasant feel. Feathers as a device to enhance the fringed elements were stitched onto the chiffon to anchor the pointed hems of the dresses and skirts emphasizing an ethereal look. The collection met with great success editorially, Penelope Tree modelled the Jacquard satin dress and chiffon jacket for Italian *Vogue* shot by David Bailey, whilst Henry Clarke photographed two kaftan-like dresses for British *Vogue*.

Top Zandra Rhodes in her dramatic quilted coat of unbleached calico printed with *Chevron Shawl*, 1970. The edges of the stylized fringed shawl print have been cut out and stitched around to show the print on either side. The calico is bagged outwards. On the body, the tasseled fringe drapes downwards. Caterine Millianaire.

Right *Chevron Shawl Print*, three-colour print on calico, Zandra Rhodes, 1970.

Opposite Dramatic quilted coat from *Chevron Shawl* collection featured in *Viva*. Photo by Art Kane, 1970.

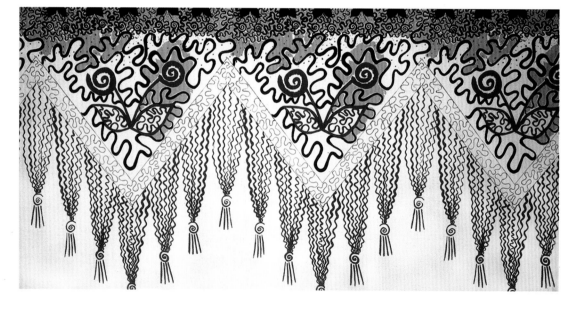

HENRY CLARKE

The National Museum of the American Indian in New York City was the sole inspiration behind the *Indian Feather* collection of textiles. You can grasp a compositional confidence from the prints, showing a maturity within Rhodes's design. The collection was composed of four prints *Indian Feather Sunspray*, *Feather and Triangle*, *Indian Feather Border*, and *Feather Border*. Rhodes recalls there were

'feathers everywhere, feathers tied on purely as adornment, feathers dyed and sewn with cross-stitch on to jackets; feathers used as edgings, as well as decoration of the clothes.'[100]

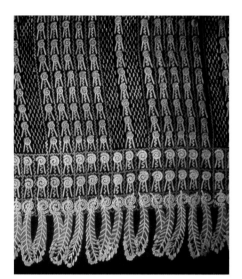

The Native American costume showed a sophistication of cut and brilliance with decorative details. Intricate patterns worked in dyed porcupine quills, cut horizontally, and used as beads, jackets made from half-inch triangles of sealskin of different shades, sewn into the finest patchwork; leather frock coats with inset embroidery in quills and feathers. Furthermore, she took in the colours of the Native Americans dress noting how somber colours were used in North America whilst tribes that lived in the South of the country under the sun used vivid colours. These were translated into directional printed textiles using black, terracotta, red, turquoise, green, white, and mustardy yellow forms of feathers, wiggles, cross hatch, cross stitch, swirls, and stripes.

Here, Rhodes continued the theme of stitching, where the print gives the impression of feathers sewn or embroidered on to the flat fabric with cross-stitches. This was a progression from her first collection of textiles through to her second, *Chevron Shawl*, where actual feathers were attached to the hem of the garments. The evolution from real feathers to printed feathers which are then cut out to create the feathered edges can be seen on the dresses, coats and tunics. Rhodes cut around every feather and hand rolled the edges herself preferring couture hand crafted practices than using a sewing machine; hand-cutting fabric would be further developed in the *Elizabethan Slashed Silk* collection. The *Indian Feather* textiles proved to be versatile as prints employed for the bodice of dresses but also as designs to suit the hem or sleeves of a dress, using the prints as borders in particular *Indian Feather Sunspray* and *Indian Feather Border*.

Above *Indian Feather Border*, four-colour print on silk chiffon, Zandra Rhodes, 1970.

Top right *Feather Border* print is used in this striking kaftan in three different colourways. The kaftans hang from yokes with ruched sleeves gathered horizontally; trimmed with velvet ribbon. 1970. Norman Eales.

Centre right *Indian Feather Sunspray*, three-colour print on silk chiffon, Zandra Rhodes, 1970.

Bottom right Indian Feather fashion sketch from Zandra Rhodes's sketchbook, circa 1970.

Opposite *Indian Feather Sunspray* Kaftan. This fashion photograph was taken for *Anan* magazine in Japan late in 1971, it featured shoes by Manolo Blahnik @ Zapata and hair by Leonard. Bishin Jumonji.

[100] Rhodes, p. 54.

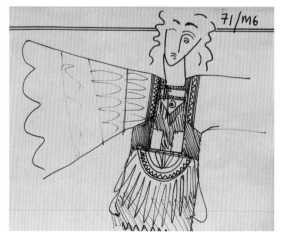

The *Elizabethan Slashed Silk* collection of spring 1971 was significant for Rhodes' further experimentation with, and manipulation of, fabric. The genesis of the *Elizabethan* Collection was again generated by her visit to the Museum of the American Indian made during Rhodes's second trip to New York in September 1970. The Native Americans and their use of natural fur and objects, such as porcupine quills, for decoration, struck her. Looking at Native American art forced Rhodes to consider her British roots, particularly the Elizabethan era, parallel to the early Native American period, with their particular treatment of textiles. Again, her academic background played a part and Rhodes visited the V&A to study Elizabethan slashed and pinked silk bodices and doublets, examining the decorative raw cuts in the fabric. In the sixteenth and seventeenth centuries, the pinking of fabric was formed with a special tool, a pinking punch, which made zigzag edges on fabric, these techniques became the inspiration for *Elizabethan Slashed Silk* collection of textiles, comprised of *Sparkle* and *Hatched* prints. The inspiration for the silhouettes of the garments fed from the shape of the print as well as being based on Native American leather tunics.

Rhodes first took the silk and cut into it by hand with a knife in the same zigzag pattern as she had seen at the V&A. The print, *Sparkle*, was initially designed around the cuts in the fabric. "The zigzag and hatched shapes were all again influenced by stitch work, the idea being that I had done blanket stitch or herringbone all round the holes."[101] Once more, Rhodes reworked the theme of stitching first seen in the prints *Knitted Circle* and *Chevron Shawl* into the collection.

The main element in the *Sparkle* print included a cigar-like shape which developed from the neon tubes and light filaments in the prints *All Over Neon* and *Mr Man*, here in a solid colour with a prominent outline, where the silk could then be cut in the middle of the shape. Rhodes recalls she "laid out the separate motifs for my sparkle print (the zigzags, the ovals, and the blanket-stitched ovals) with a strange combined formality that had something of Tudor symmetry about it."[102] A visit to Hampton Court, the Tudor palace once the home of Henry VIII, assisted Rhodes with the final layout of the print, as she looked to the zigzag brickwork of the chimneys and the gunroom with its weapons hung in a crisscross pattern.

The liberation of fashion from the restrictions of protocol in the mid '60s and '70s,

Right Grace Coddington models Zandra Rhodes's *Elizabethan Slashed Silk* collection. The dress is formed of cream silk combining hand-printed *Sparkle* and *Indian Feather Border* designs. The silk is slashed leaving cut raw edges, some edges bound with silk rouleaux. *Vogue,* March 1971, Guy Bourdin/ Vogue ©The Condé Nast Publications Ltd.

Opposite page *Sparkle* dress in silk chiffon. A fashion shoot for *Anan* magazine in Japan. The model's makeup is inspired by Zandra Rhodes's own of the period with plucked eyebrows replaced by glitter dots and rhinestones, 1971. Bishin Jumonji.

[101] Rhodes, p. 68.

[102] Rhodes, p. 68.

zandra rhodes

however, allowed Rhodes the liberty to experiment with historic textile techniques using the pinking technique to leave hem edges unfinished and slashing parts of the fabric. Slashing into the fabric also anticipated by six years the hard-edged DIY Punk look later in the decade.[103] The shape of the *Sparkle* print inspired the silhouettes of the dresses as well as the animal skin shapes that Rhodes had seen in the Museum of the American Indian and experimented with in her *Indian Feathers* collection. The collection was modelled and styled by Grace Coddington and photographed by Guy Bourdin in a dynamic shoot for *Vogue*. The resulting spread, entitled 'Scissored Silks' stated, 'Zandra Rhodes' dresses are the airiest lightly printed silks, got at by a pair of mad scissors. Blouses, shifts and knickerbockers are pinked at the edges and seams, castellated, slashed into waves of length, cut in slits and Vs, so that every piece streams in tiers of points and curves.'[104]

The streaming, slashed, *Elizabethan* collection was a milestone for Rhodes. She staged her first fashion show with these designs at Angelo Donghia's town house in New York. It was a direct attempt to illustrate much more than a collection of dresses. Its aim was to show how Rhodes's ideas went beyond fashion and textiles extending to a total look with jewellery by Mick Milligan, and Leonard flying over from London to style the hair; establishing her as a significant name in design. The show, entitled *The Fantasy World of Zandra Rhodes*, was organized by the doyenne of American Fashion publicists Eleanor Lambert, and the audience was composed of America's most influential people in fashion, especially the 'High Priestess' Diana Vreeland and the 'King', Halston. Janis Joplin blasted over the stereo to set the mood, whilst the models strutted throughout the apartment on the shimmering painted floor. The newspapers noted the following day:

'Her fantasy clothes and Rhodes's own personal rainbow appearance are enough of a combination to make an indelible impression on anyone. Fashion experts are talking about her as a truly original talent in a category with Giorgio di Saint Angelo, Karl Lagerfeld, Ossie Clark, Jean Muir, and Thea Porter. The dresses themselves have long floaty skirts slashed into ribbon streamers, zigzag hemlines… pinked edges and loose kaftan-like shapes with raw slits cut into some of the figures in the print. Her slit silks are quite unusual and one of those ideas that made me think when I saw the dresses, "Why didn't someone do it before?" Each dress takes on an unusual but graceful look when air gets under it – the slits open just a bit.'[105]

Below *Sparkle* print slashed chiffon kaftan, priced £150 at Piero de Monzi, 1971.

Opposite An exuberant image of the *Elizabethan Slashed Silk* collection dresses in silk and silk chiffon. Italian *Vogue* February 1974. Courtesy Chris von Wagenheim.

[103] Rhodes's use of the slashing technique in this collection is in part about creating a regular, repeating decorative pattern that is aesthetically pleasing, but when she reworked the slashing motif in 1977 for her Punk-inspired *Conceptual Chic* collection it was the antithesis of this.

[104] *Vogue* (British), March 1971.

[105] *The Philadelphia Enquirer*, 4 May 1971.

In 1971, Sekers Silk Pty, Ltd, known as Sekers Australia, launched an exclusive range of twelve prints designed by Rhodes. Miki Sekers and his cousin Tomi de Gara founded Sekers Silks in 1938 in West Cumberland, to manufacture high-quality silk and rayon fabrics for the fashion trade. Following the war, couturiers such as Christian Dior, Edward Molyneux, Pierre Cardin and Givenchy used Sekers fabrics. Sekers partners, Mr. and Mrs. Bandi Kaldor established Sekers Australia in the 1950s to import Miki Sekers's woven textiles into Australia. The business was successful for many years but around 1965 the tariffs for import rose, making the business unpromising, leaving the Kaldors to branch out commissioning and marketing their prints often produced in Japan. The business retained the Sekers brand name, shifting their focus from woven to printed textiles, at which they excelled.

Over a two-year period Mrs. Vera Kaldor, Fashion Director of Sekers Silk Pty, Ltd watched Rhodes gain notoriety for her innovative textiles, prompting her to visit Rhodes in London and subsequently commission her to create exclusive designs for Sekers Australia. The official Press Release from Sekers Australia stated:

'Her hair is usually multi coloured, like some exotic bird of paradise. Make-up can be anything on Zandra provided it does not match. Zandra believes you can put things in bad taste and make them good taste – as long as you know the difference and are not pretending.'[106]

It was Rhodes's sassy comments and her bold aesthetic, a point of differentiation that captured attention and rendered her truly

Top Sekers Australia advertisement announcing 'zany Zandra Rhodes' 'Off the Peg' fashions made from her exclusive Sekers textile designs. *Australian Woman's Weekly* 28 July 1971.

Bottom Rhodes's textiles for Sekers Australia dramatically displayed in Myer's shop window, August 1971.

Opposite Rhodes's own label textile and dresses in Myer's shop window, July/August 1971.

[106] Sekers Silk Pty, Ltd. Zandra Rhodes archive.

[107] Sekers Australia and Farmer and Co Invitation to preview reception, Zandra Rhodes archive.

[108] Myer advertisement, *Herald*, Melbourne, Australia, 7 August 1971.

[109] Myer advertisement, *Western Advocate*, Bathurst, Australia, 8 August 1971.

[110] Sekers advertisement, Zandra Rhodes archive.

original. The prints were sold by the yard, for Australian women to sew their own fashions from or in off-the-peg garments, some made up from *Vogue* patterns, others inspired by Rhodes's silhouettes in bubble and kaftan-like shapes. A departure from Rhodes's own line of 'new couture' textiles, these were mass-produced and printed on fabrics such as voiles, polyesters, sateens, and fine jerseys.

Sekers Australia in conjunction with two major department stores in Australia, Myer and Farmer's, and the *Australian Women's Weekly* magazine, heavily promoted the Sekers/Zandra Rhodes line of printed textiles. A preview reception was held in Sydney at Farmer and Co, the invitation reading, 'see the magic that happens when zany Zandra's genius sets Australia's top fashion talents on fire.'[107] Rhodes's collection of readymade fashions were paraded daily for a week each at Farmer's in Sydney and Myer Emporium in Melbourne during the month of August, with Rhodes made special appearances at each store. Advertisements taken out in newspapers across the country stated:

'Zandra Rhodes… couturier! Shock waves out of England… whose zany, wildly beautiful designs are worn by jet-setters everywhere.'[108] 'The colours are just breathtaking and the design- revolutionary'.[109]

"Zandra Rhodes is a designer? She's a bird of paradise…She's a shock wave out of England and she'll charm you out of your mind. She's 1971 No.1 creator. She has a poet's eye, an original paintbrush and some enchanted scissors. She whips up ravishing things of rainbows and dreams…The astonishing fabrics she decorated for nobody but Sekers are here."[110] Rhodes's revolutionary designed fabrics were sold by the yard priced from Aus $2 to Aus $4.50, whilst the ready-to-wear garments were priced Aus $10 for a drawstring blouse, Aus $35 for a dress and Aus $39 for an outfit of long dress and matching hot pants. Sekers/Zandra Rhodes fabric was available at all the Myer and Farmer stores whilst the ready-to-wear garments were in select locations.

The expansive department store windows at Myer's in Sydney were given over to promoting Sekers/Zandra Rhodes fabrics, which were draped from floor to ceiling to striking effect, and her own label couture fashions and Sekers textiles were made up into fashionable dresses on mannequins amongst stylized trees. A large photographic shoot was also arranged for advertising purposes as well as features in *Australian Woman's Weekly* magazine displaying the innovative prints made up into flowing dresses. The exclusive collection of textiles for Sekers again called on Rhodes's signature motifs of wiggles, chain link stitching, snail flowers, cross-hatching, wiggle tassels, and stitched flowers. Made into a myriad of bright colourways; there was a choice that would suit various customers' tastes. The Sekers commission made Rhodes a household name in Australia, a country to which she should would return time and again. One of Rhodes's most famous later collections of textiles from 1974 was based on Ayers rock and her fascination with the landscapes of Central Australia.

Top *All Over Flower Power 2*, four-colour print, Zandra Rhodes for Sekers Australia, 1971. The print is similar to that designed for &Vice Versa wallpapers, here the wiggles are more pronounced and interesting colourways are used to breathe new life into the textile.

From left Fashion shoot with Rhodes's Sekers Australia's textiles made up into garments inspired by Zandra Rhodes's own label dresses and kaftans, July 1971.

Top *Wiggle Tassel Triangle*,
four-colour print, Zandra Rhodes
for Sekers Australia, 1971.

Bottom *Knitted Flower and
Circles*, four-colour print, Zandra
Rhodes for Sekers Australia, 1971.

The *Button Flower* Collection of Autumn 1971 was a crucial collection of textiles and clothes for Zandra Rhodes. She transformed elements of the two-dimensional print into the three-dimensional as well as designed clothes that did not correspond to the form of the print, breaking away from her established process. J.& J. Stern Ltd., Button Manufacturers, 5 Great Chapel Street, London W1, (no longer on the premises) where Rhodes shopped for buttons ignited the forms for this collection of textiles. On a particular trip to J.& J. Stern, she purchased simple flower and geometric shaped buttons admiring the way the buttons were arranged in the shop but also their presentation, attached to cards with little pinked shapes of coloured fabric around each sample. Other influences working alongside the flower-shaped buttons, such as old copies of Paris broderie magazines purchased from Parisian flea markets, showed lace, crochet, embroidery techniques, and designs.

Rhodes' aim was to design a flower print that broke with tradition using the fancy buttons from J. & J. Stern in the studio. She drew flowers like buttons stitched on to the fabric; the buttons being the centre of the flower with modern, bold Henri Matisse-like shapes for the petals. The first print *Buttonflower* came to fruition. Developing the button, flower and broderie ideas further Rhodes looked to eighteenth-century paintings by Jean-Honoré Fragonard and François Boucher in the Wallace Collection, London. Within the paintings, the wealth of detail in the costume depicted the decorative elements: frills, buttons, bows, lace, and flowers. Rhodes being particularly drawn to the frills in the overskirts and sleeves. The wiggly and frilly features combined with the buttonflower translated to the prints *Frilly Flower* and then *Frilly*; the prints being one-way or two-way designs and highly detailed, hand-printed in primary colours.

For the corresponding clothes designs the intention was to break away from the flat print being the guiding principle in the silhouette, letting the shaping and draping practices Rhodes experienced in Paris take the lead. The interpreted two-dimensional buttons, bows, and frills were then printed and cut out as decorative three-dimensional elements placed on coats, dresses, skirts, and overalls. The three-dimensional buttonflower motifs were placed on the shoulder of her famous dinosaur coat (a skilfully shaped oversized felt coat with pinked seams on the outside) and other garments in what Rhodes called the Matisse style after his colourful painting *La Blouse Roumaine*, in which the figure wears a blouse with floral motifs on the sleeves. Skirts for the collection pared with shorter jackets were put together in a manner of pleated frilled layers that matched the *Frilly Flower* and *Frilly* prints; the pleating sprayed in many directions. Here Rhodes created her own frills stretching the edges of silken jersey as they were being oversewn to produce a lettuce effect. The *Buttonflower* collection of textiles were hand printed on felt, silk, chiffon, satin, and crepe showing a mastery of printing abilities.

The leading fashion magazines again supported the *Buttonflower* collection editorially with Clive Arrowsmith and David Bailey shooting ensembles from the collection for *Vogue*. At this time, Anne Knight who bought Rhodes's designs for the Odyssey Room, left Fortnum & Mason to pursue her career and Rhodes was left without a London stockist. She quickly met the owner of the small but renowned boutique, Piero de Monzi on Fulham Road, and struck a deal with the boutique to exclusively sell her collections. The boutique also had an art gallery attached to it, The D.M. Gallery. Here Rhodes staged her first London fashion show, a small intimate affair, which included an exhibition of her framed fashion drawings. Anjelica Huston, then 16, and Beatrice Wells modelled in that first British show. Rhodes had finally realized her vision of taking her hand printed textiles into the fashion world but also gaining respect as an artist within that context.

Broderie Image which Zandra Rhodes purchased from a Paris flea market, 1971.

Right and below Two *Buttonflower* fashion sketches from Zandra Rhodes's sketchbook, circa 1971-2.

Far right *Buttonflower*, three-colour print on silk chiffon, Zandra Rhodes, 1971. The corresponding garments for this collection were featured in *Vogue* and *Anan* in Japan where Rhodes staged a fashion show. The Japanese market took well to the naïve/Pop style of the bright buttonflower print and stiff felt 'Dinosaur' coats with appliquéd buttonflower motifs on the shoulder.

Below left Fashion sketch from Zandra Rhodes's sketchbook showing buttonflower ideas, circa 1971-2.

Below centre Black and white sketch of dinosaur coat from Zandra Rhodes's sketchbook, 1972.

Below right Zandra Rhodes in *Buttonflower* dinosaur coat with Mick Milligan Rhinestone buttons in her hair, London, 1972.

Opposite Penelope Tree in Ivory felt Buttonflower Dinosaur Coat with buttonflower appliqué and pinked seams with matching offset halo hat. *Vogue,* September 1971. David Bailey/Vogue©The Condé Nast Publications Ltd.

* * * * * * * * * *

Zandra Rhodes was awarded *Designer of the Year* by the English Fashion Trade in 1972, the same year she staged her first London catwalk show at the famous Roundhouse Theatre in Camden. This theatrically spectacular production at midnight captured the attention of the press on both sides of the Atlantic and led Rhodes to produce her fashion shows in New York at the famous Circle in the Square Theatre in 1973 and 1974. Rhodes's position in the fashion world was such that Princess Anne wore a Rhodes creation for her official engagement portrait, forever captured by the lens of Norman Parkinson.

Rhodes also realized a dream of opening a freestanding Zandra Rhodes boutique in the exclusive neighbourhood of Mayfair in London with Anne Knight and Ronnie Stirling as partners.[111] The interior transformed – by Rhodes and Richard Holley into a patterned paradise of printed satin feathered prints combined with specially designed bronze foil wallpaper (inspired by her early work for &Vice Versa) – completed the look. Rhodes's exceptional interior design proved a popular format and was adapted for in-store boutiques at Bloomingdale's in New York City and Marshall Fields in Chicago, with the *Zandra Rhodes Shop* opening in Harrods the following year in 1976. Rhodes was given the prestigious honour of Royal Designer for Industry in 1974 by HRH Prince Philip, the youngest designer to be presented with such an award at the time. The *Conceptual Chic* collection introduced torn and slashed jersey dresses and ensembles with diamanté, chains and safety pins, a departure from Rhodes's printed work, landing her large features in *People* and *Newsweek* magazines. Following the overall success of her label, she branched out to design her first collection of lingerie featuring pleated silk robes and delicate printed nightwear for Eve Stillman (a New York based company). Since then, Rhodes's textiles have decorated everything from swimwear, handbags, tents, wellington boots, linings of fur coats, shoes, hosiery, fragrance bottles, and make-up packaging to striking effect.

Her first collections and art school experiments shown within this book were only the beginning for Rhodes whose career has spanned over forty years. Her early textile designs from 1961 to 1971 show the growth and development of a young designer who achieved a unique visual language with the intelligent use of colour and imagery that is still relevant today. At the RCA, Rhodes began her illustrious career becoming one of the most prolific and lasting

designers of her generation. There she formulated her ideas about textiles and perfected her printing and designing skills, in the studio from dawn until dusk. Former Rector of the RCA, Christopher Frayling, in his speech to award Rhodes an honourary doctorate in 1986, stated Rhodes was convinced of three things in 1964, her graduation year.

"Her works should stand comparison with that of other painters and sculptors; there was more to life than designing fabrics for other people to cut about; and most dramatic of all she was part of the canvas, she would become a walking, talking research and development department."[112] Rhodes realized the three goals she set out to accomplish as Ruskin wrote using her hand, heart, and head with an 'original paintbrush and enchanted scissors'.[113]

Right Zandra Rhodes with signature make-up of glitter dots and rounded rouge on her cheeks with chunky faux coral necklace and diamanté brooches, c.1971/2.

Opposite Silk chiffon *Buttonflower* bubble dress, *Vogue*, October 1971. Clive Arrowsmith/Vogue ©The Condé Nast Publications Ltd.

[111] Rhodes's freestanding boutique on Grafton Street combined all of Rhodes's design output under one roof. A client could purchase Rhodes's textiles, dresses, accessories, handbags, furnishing fabric and other decorative elements for the home.

[112] Royal College of Art Archive.

[113] Sekers advertisement, Zandra Rhodes archive

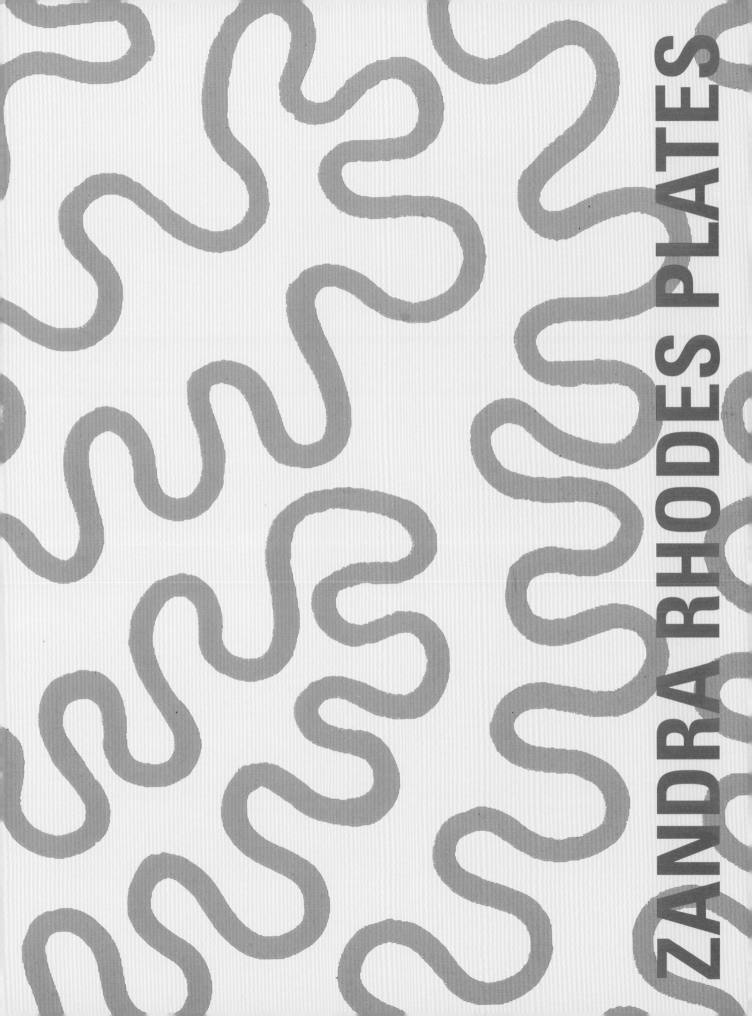

ZANDRA RHODES PLATES

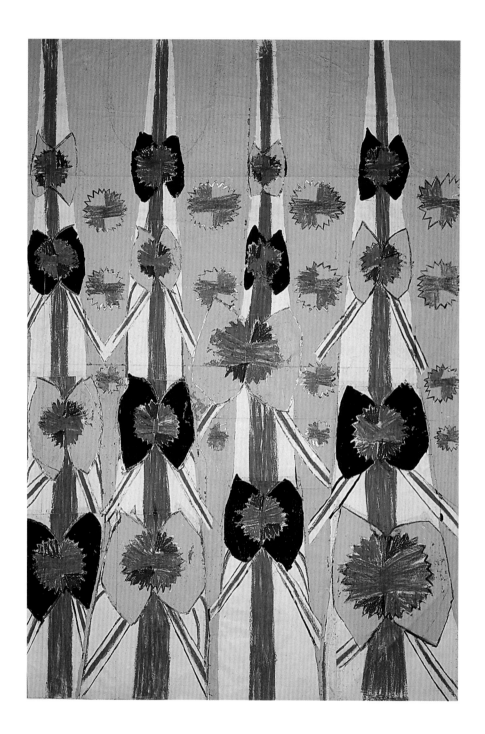

1 Left *Medal Bows*, panel print design for a full-length garment designed at the RCA in 1964. See the cut out armholes at the top of the print where Zandra Rhodes tried it on to see how the design worked on the body.

2 Opposite *Top Brass*, eight-colour print on cotton sateen produced as a furnishing fabric for Heal's, displayed in Zandra Rhodes's diploma show at the RCA, 1964. Based on the theme of medals stemming from David Hockney's paintings using decorative medals.

3 Left Moiré *Medal* panel, four-colour print for white cotton velvet, RCA, 1963-4. Two prints hung in Zandra Rhodes's diploma show are based on the moiré design of this panel.

4 Opposite Design idea for *Medals*, gouache on shiny paper with paint, RCA, 1963-4.

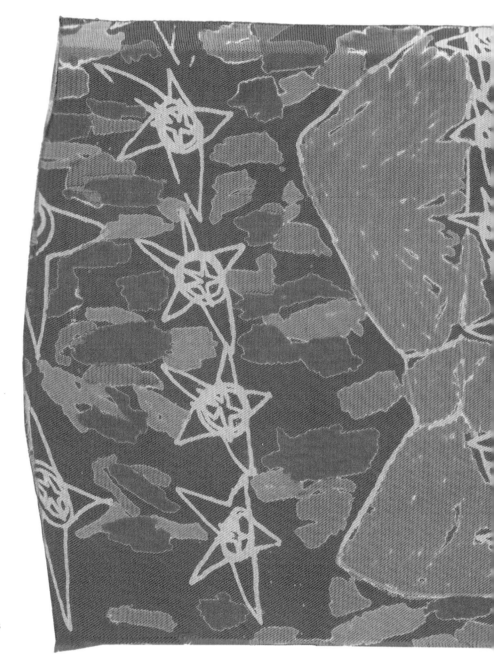

5 *Medal, Bows and Stars*, experimental four-colour discharge print on purple dyed fine silk twill, displayed in Zandra Rhodes's diploma show at the RCA, 1964. The bold printed outline around the stars has been left out of the print. (Shown here on its side – view with bow uppermost.)

6 Next page, top left *Medal, Bows and Stars*, three-colour experimental print on fine silk twill, displayed in Zandra Rhodes's diploma show at the RCA, 1964. Here Rhodes takes away elements of the original print such as paint splodge-like shapes and the colourful bows.

7 Next page, centre left *Medal, Bows and Stars*, original four-colour print on fine silk twill, displayed in Zandra Rhodes's diploma show at the RCA, 1964

8 Next page, bottom left *Medal, Bows and Stars*, three-colour experimental print on fine silk twill, RCA, 1964. Here Zandra Rhodes leaves the bold printed outline around the stars, making the bows in the print more pronounced.

9 Next page, top right *Medal, Bows and Stars*, experimental one-colour discharge print on violet-dyed fine silk twill, RCA, 1964.

10 Next page, centre right *Medal, Bows and Stars*, three-colour experimental print on fine silk twill, RCA, 1964. Here Zandra Rhodes used the bold lines of print leaving out the fine lines. RCA, 1964.

11 Next page, bottom right *Medal, Bows and Stars*, three-colour experimental print on dyed fine silk twill, RCA, 1964.

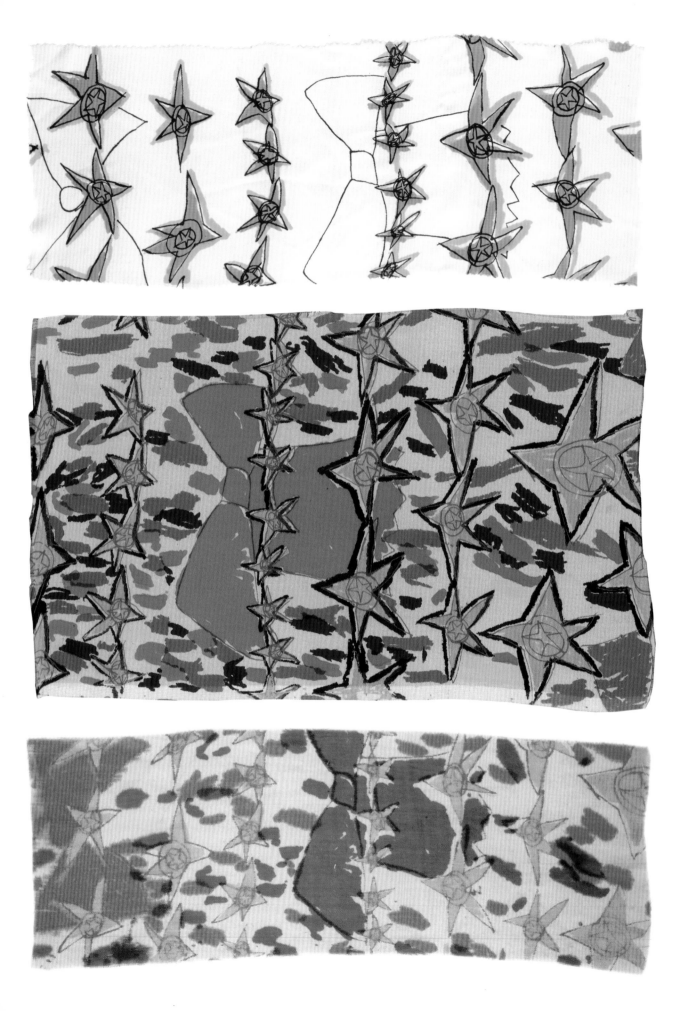

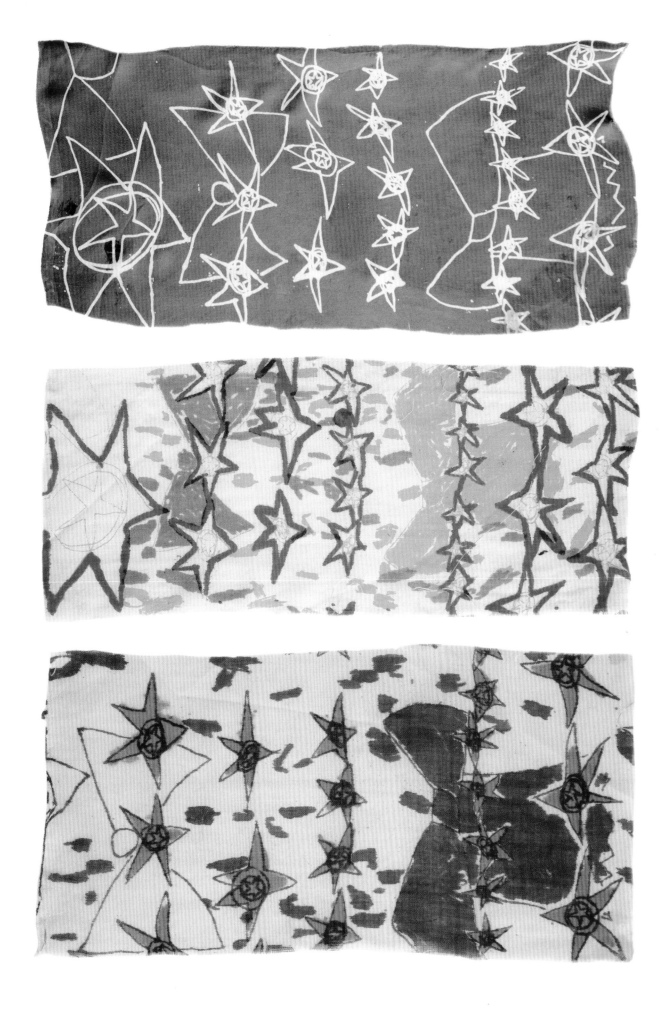

12 *Medal, Bows and Stars*,
experimental one-colour
discharge print on black
fine silk twill, RCA, 1964.

13 *Medal, Bows and Stars,*
three-colour experimental
print on fine silk twill, RCA,
1964. Here Zandra Rhodes
takes away elements of the
original print such as brush
mark shapes.

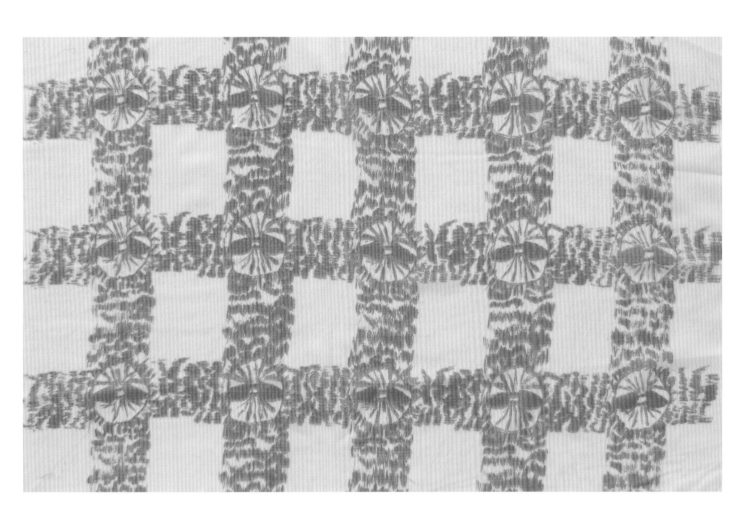

14 Top left Paper design of *Medal
Ribbon Check* print, RCA, 1964,
with moiré effect.

15 Bottom left *Medal Ribbon
Check*, experimental swatch of
two-colour print on pink crepe,
RCA, 1964.

16 Above *Medal Ribbon Check*,
two-colour print on wool lawn
challis, displayed in Zandra
Rhodes's diploma show at the
RCA, 1964. Based on Rhodes's
them of medals.

17 Next page *Medal Ribbon Check*, three-colour
experimental swatch printed on wool challis, RCA, 1964.

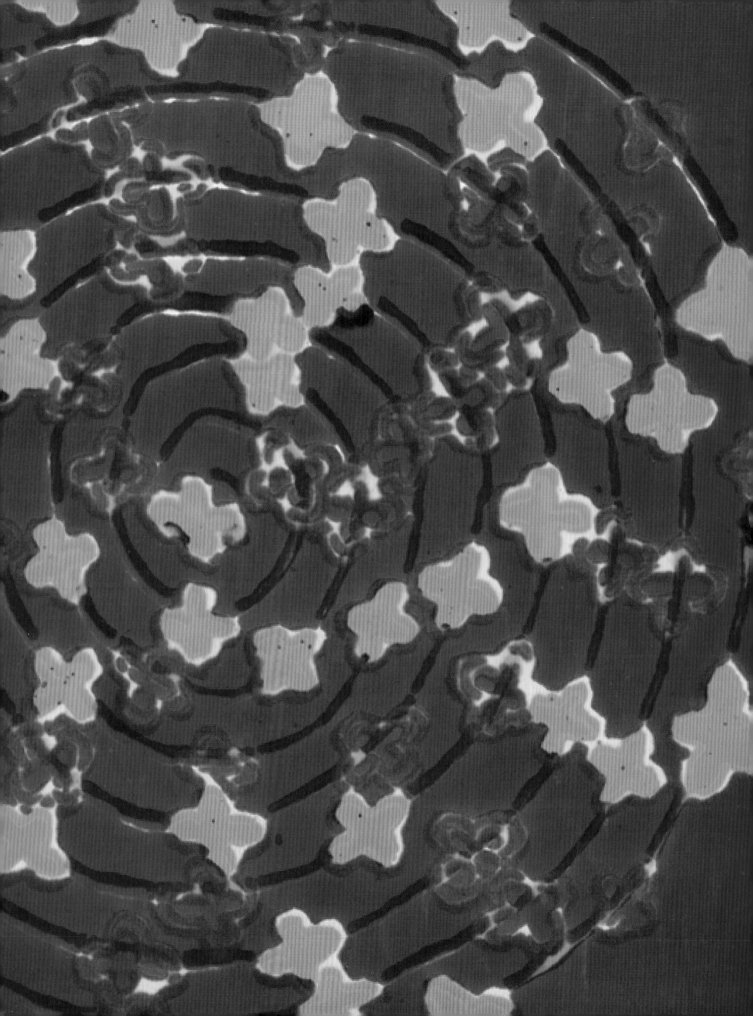

18 Previous page *Spiral Flowers*, experimental three-colour discharge print on blue silk, RCA, 1964.

19 Right *Spiral Flowers*, one-colour print on white silk, RCA, 1964. An experimental print, this colourway was featured in Rhodes's diploma show.

20 Bottom left *Spiral Flowers*, experimental three-colour discharge print on dyed green silk, RCA, 1964. Based on the design of an Iznik vase from the sixteenth century in the V&A's ceramics collection.

21 Bottom right *Spiral Flowers*, three-colour discharge print on yellow silk, displayed in Zandra Rhodes's diploma show at the CA, 1964. Rhodes was photographed for the cover of the *Sunday Times Magazine* wearing this print in a dress made by her mother.

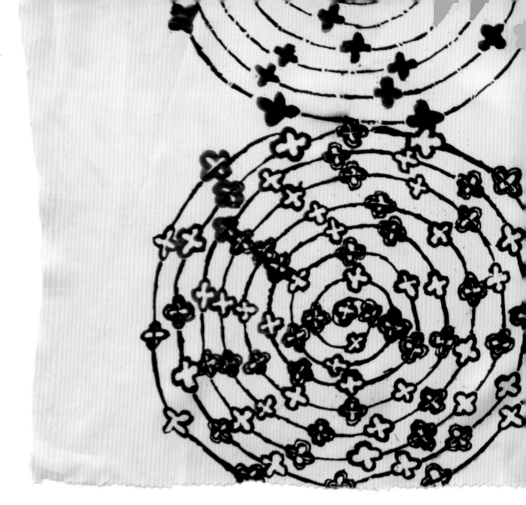

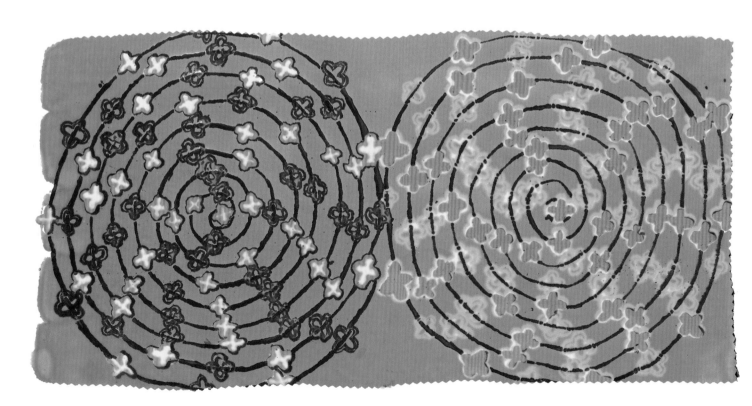

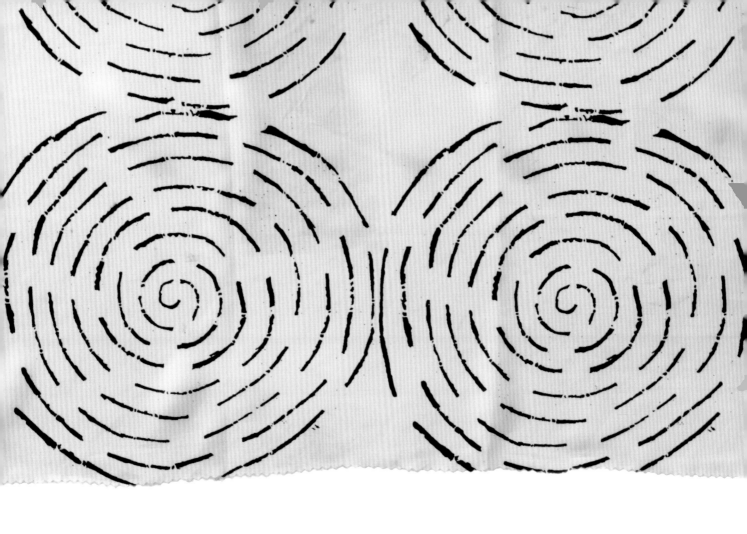
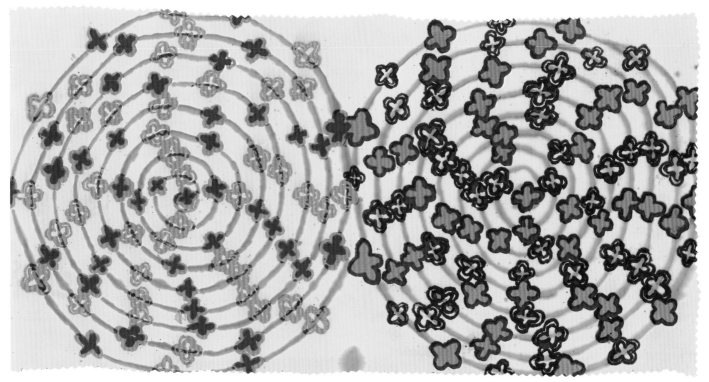

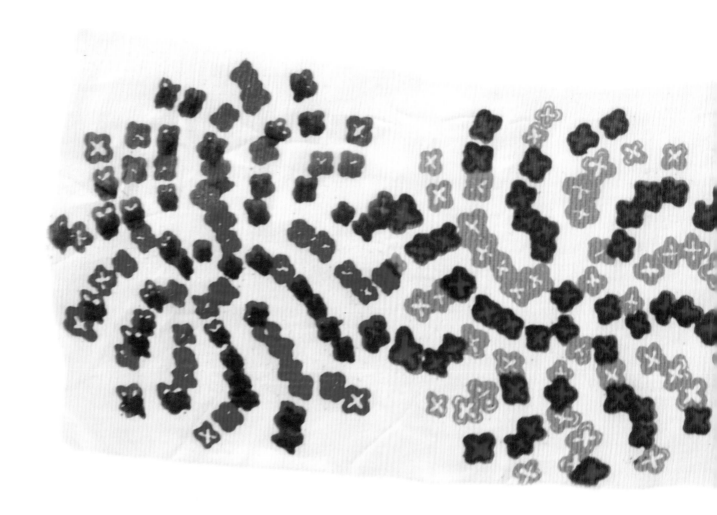

22 *Spiral Flowers* experiment,
three-colour print on white
silk chiffon, RCA, 1964. Rhodes
takes away the swirling dotted
lines from the print giving it
a more whimsical feel.

23 Next page *Spiral Flowers*, experimental three-colour
discharge print on black silk, RCA, 1964.

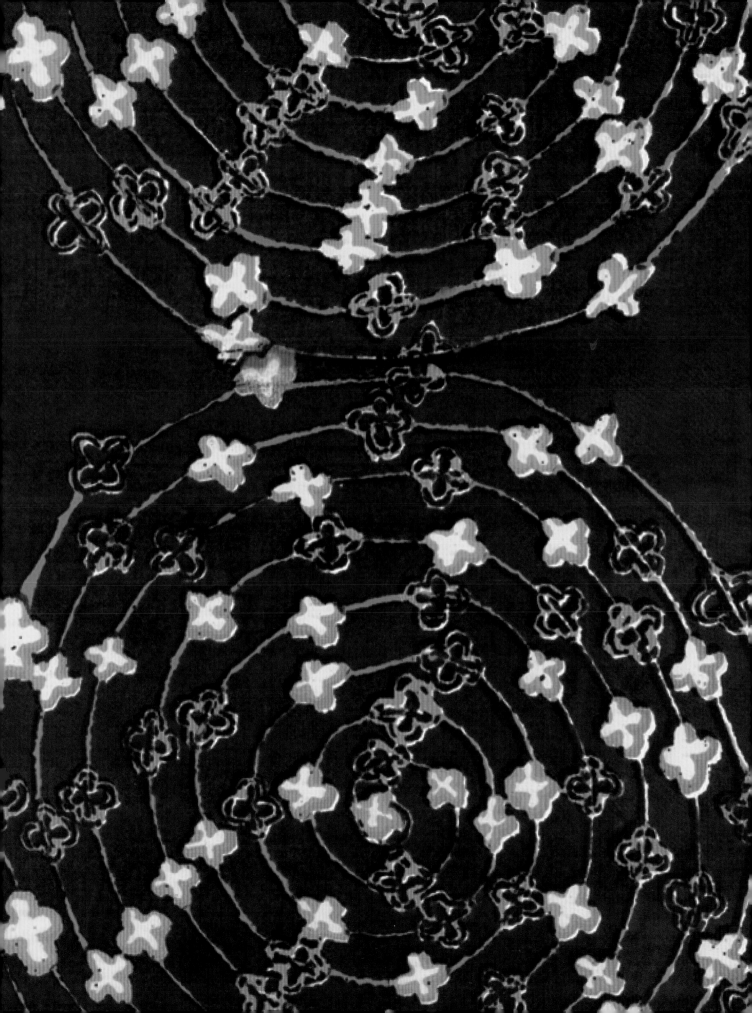

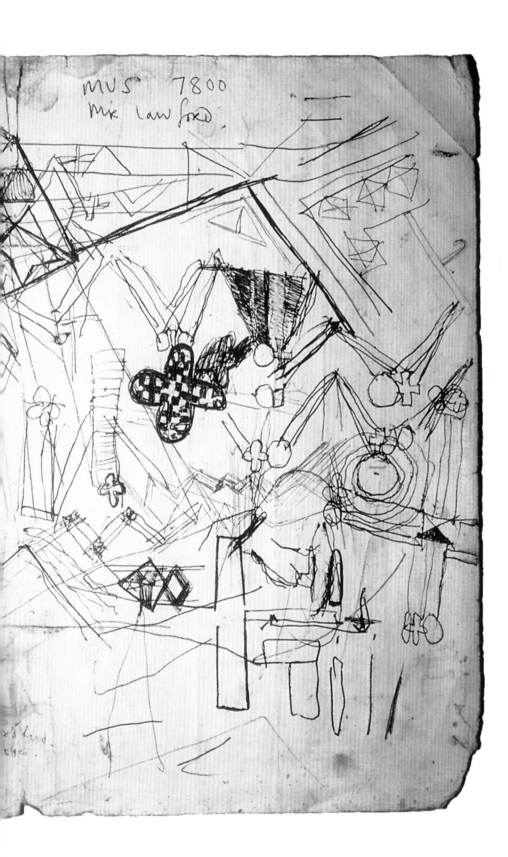

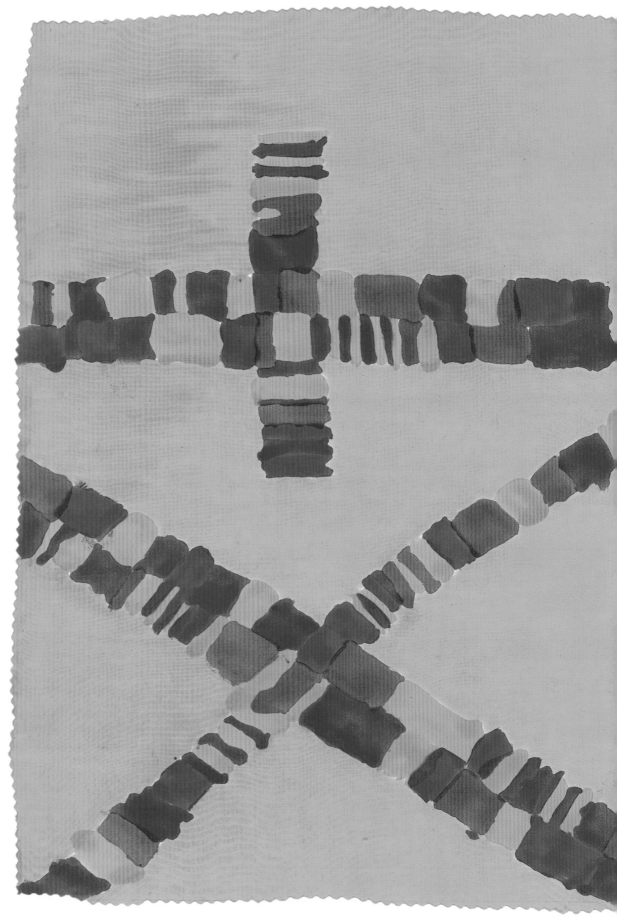

27 Flag experiment, three-colour print on dyed brown parachute silk, RCA, 1962.

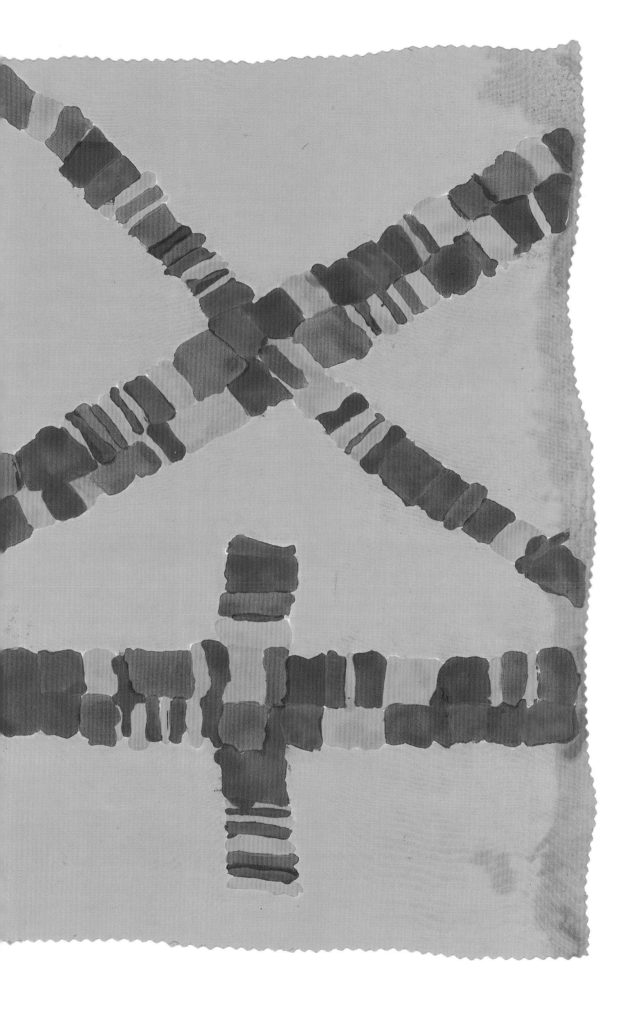

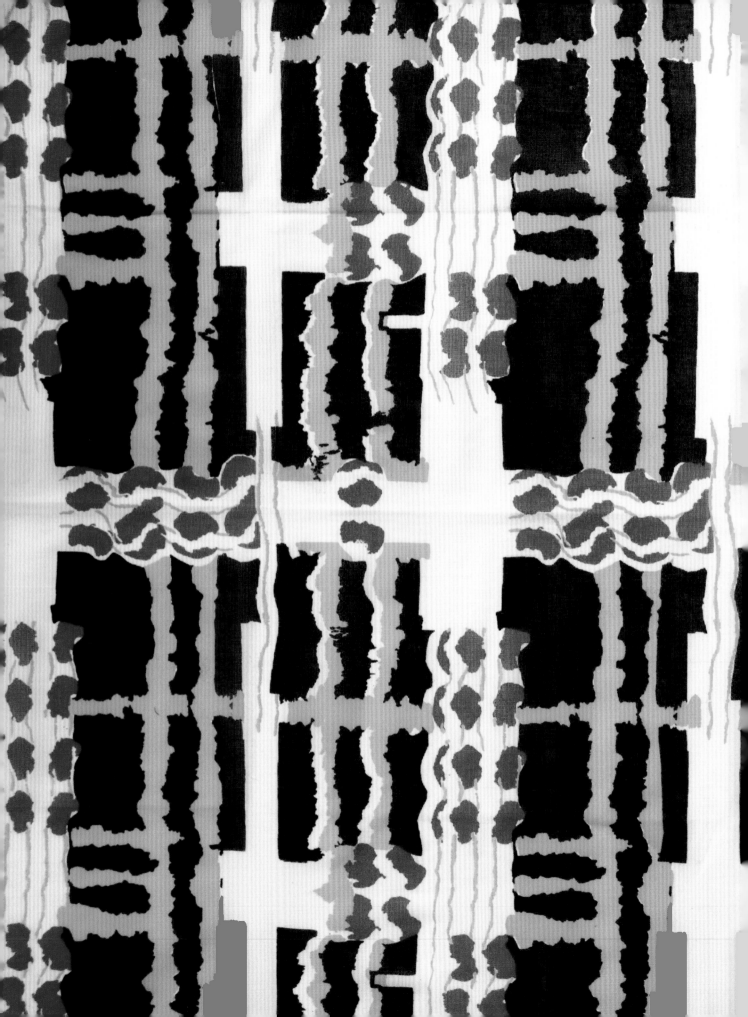

28 Previous page Torn collage design, inspired by Zandra Rhodes's experiments with flags, RCA, 1962.

29 Below *Comic* silk organza fabric scrap, RCA, 1964

30 Opposite *Comic* design on paper using dots and explosions, RCA, 1962-4

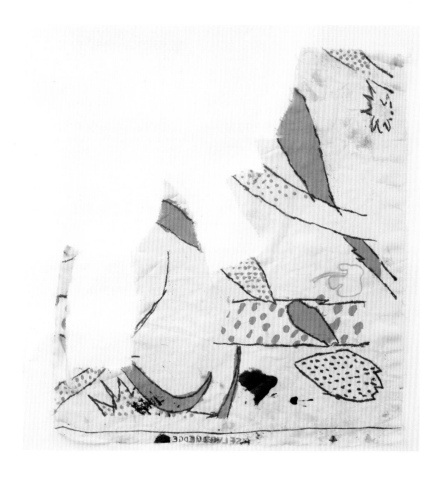

31 *Comic* check design using explosions, RCA, 1962-4, pastel and wax crayon on paper.

32 *Gala* seven-colour print on cotton produced as a furnishing fabric for Heal's, 1964. The textile combines elements of two of Zandra Rhodes's prints from her RCA diploma show; comic explosions and medal, stars and bows. V&A Images/ Victoria and Albert Museum.

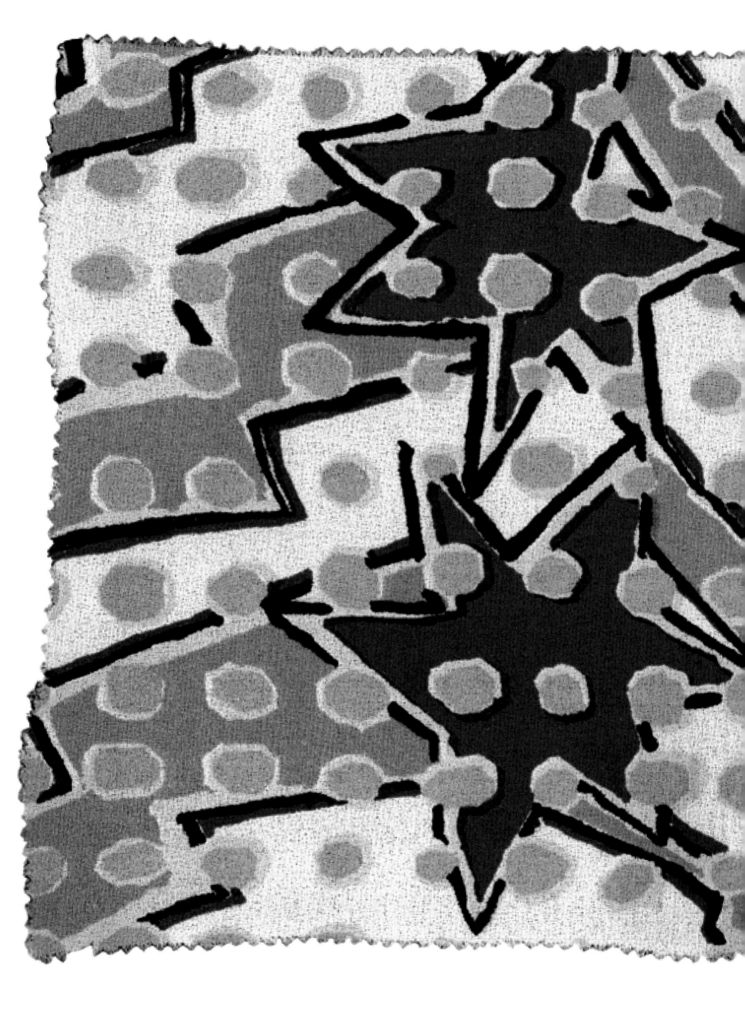

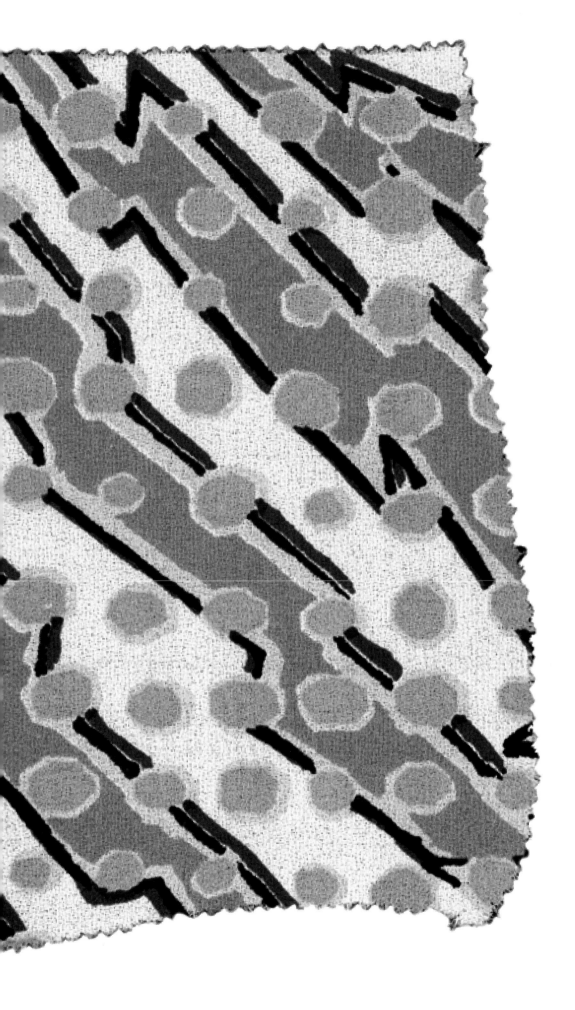

33 *Superman Star*, five-colour print on crepe, first designed at the RCA, 1962-4, used in a mini dress as the bodice and sleeve cuffs in 1968 for Zandra Rhodes's label with Sylvia Ayton.

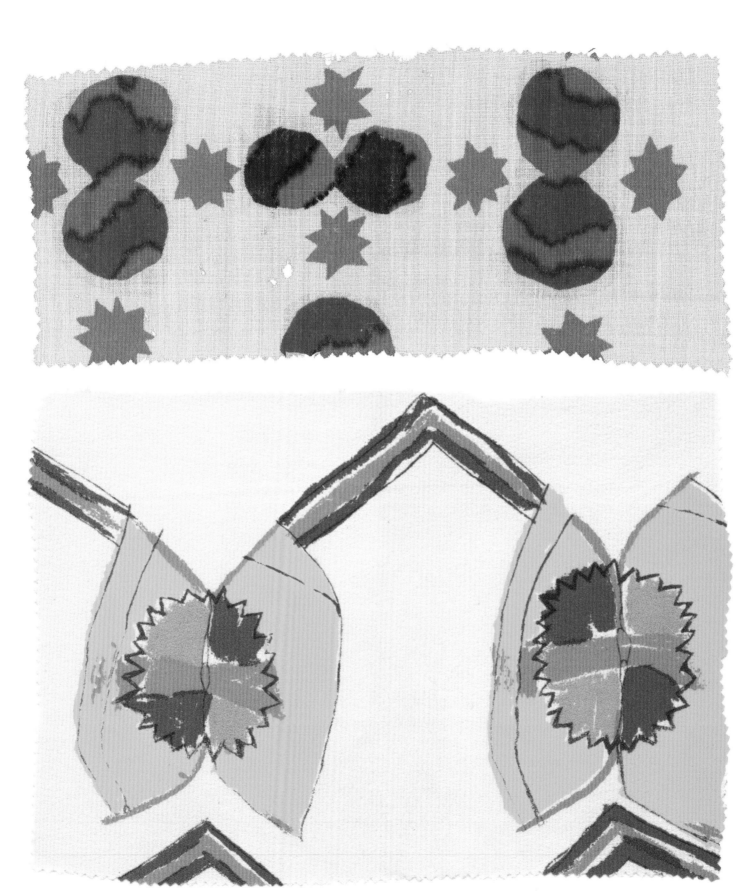

34 Previous page, top left *Starburst*, three-colour print on yellow wool challis, displayed in Zandra Rhodes's diploma show at the RCA in 1964. The print was included in Rhodes's first collection of prints for design duo Foale and Tuffin in 1965.

35 Previous page, bottom left *Zigzag Medal Bows,* five-colour print on rayon crepe for Foale and Tuffin, 1965. Based on an earlier panel design Zandra Rhodes created at the RCA this incarnation has been simplified to suit the label's needs. It was made into a trendy halterneck jumpsuit and photographed by Helmut Newton for British *Vogue* the same year, the first of Rhodes's prints to be featured in the magazine.

36 Previous page, right *Roses and Explosions* paper design, RCA, 1962-3. Zandra Rhodes cut out photographs of roses from gardening catalogues placing comic explosions around them.

37/38 Right and Opposite *Diamond and Roses*, four-colour print on crepe, first designed at the RCA 1961-1964, later used in Zandra Rhodes's first collection of textiles, *Knitted Circle*, for her eponymous line in 1969.

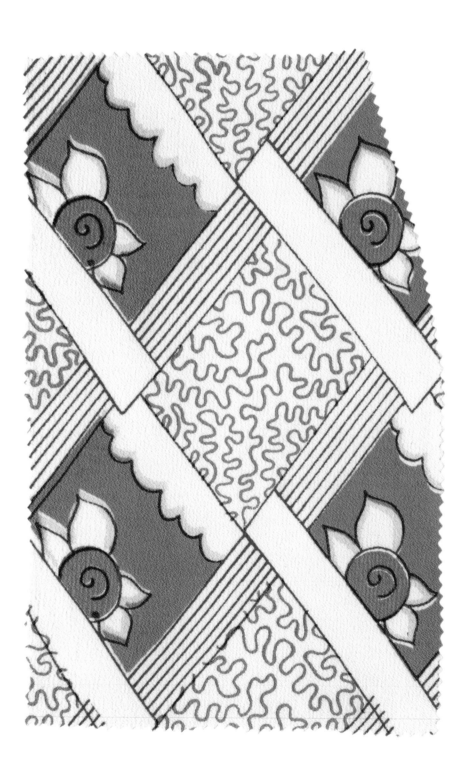

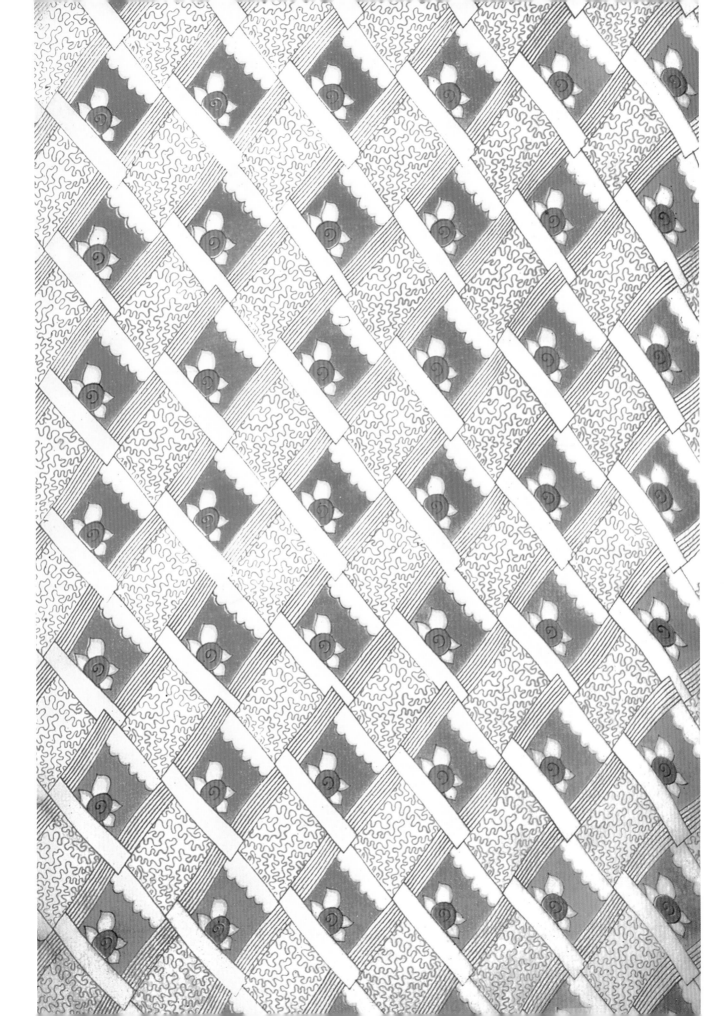

39 Top *Rainbow*, four-colour print on white crepe for Foale and Tuffin, 1965.

40 Bottom *Rainbow*, four-colour print on white crepe for Foale and Tuffin, 1965. This print was made into an A-line knee-length skirt and photographed by Helmut Newton for British *Vogue* along with the halterneck *Zigzag Medal Bows* jumpsuit.

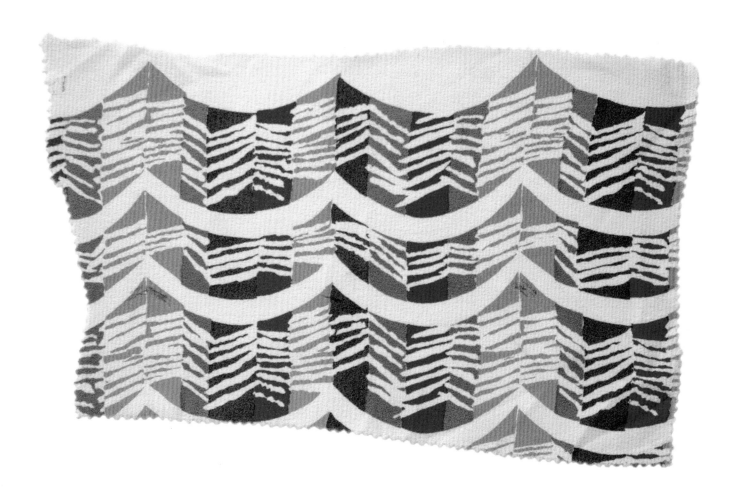

41 *Step Up Stars*, Op Art inspired three-colour print on white rayon satin for Foale and Tuffin, 1965.

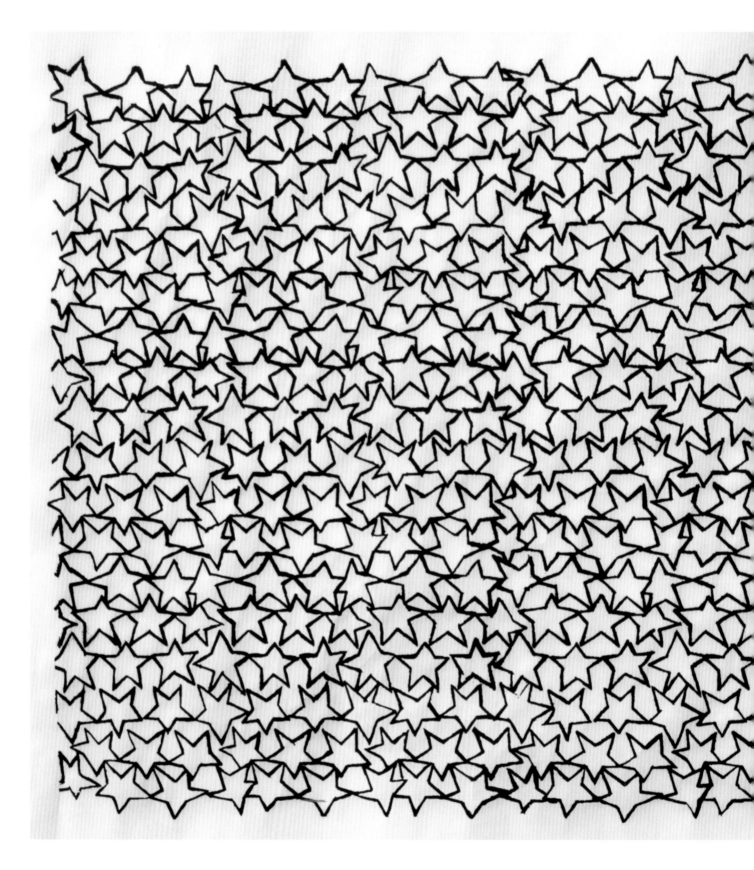

42 *Stars*, one-colour print
on rayon crepe for
Foale and Tuffin, 1964.

43 Next page *Stars*, one-colour print on rayon crepe for
Foale and Tuffin, 1964.

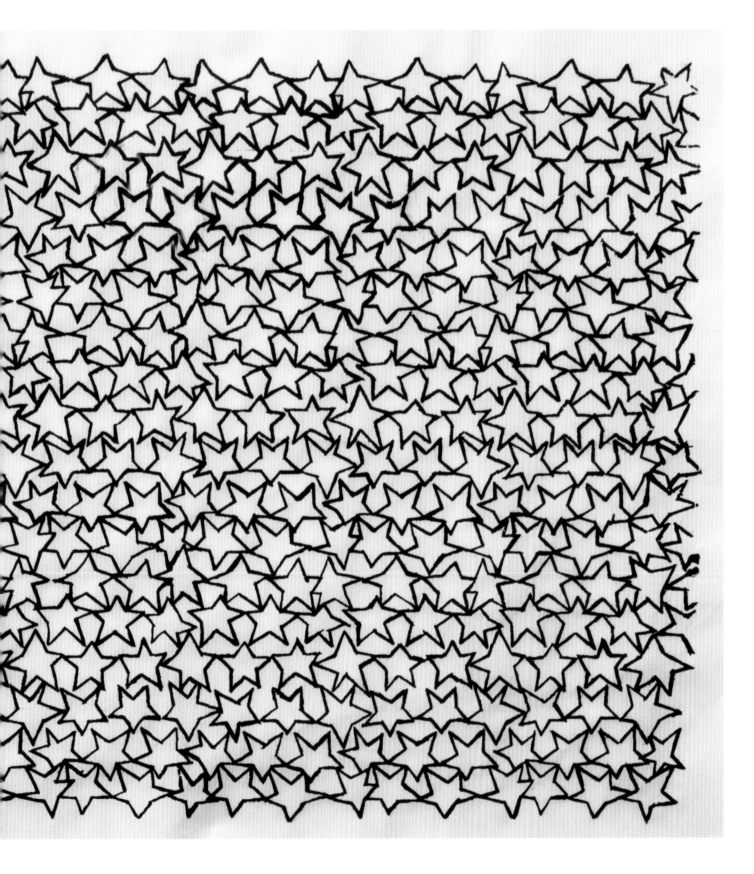

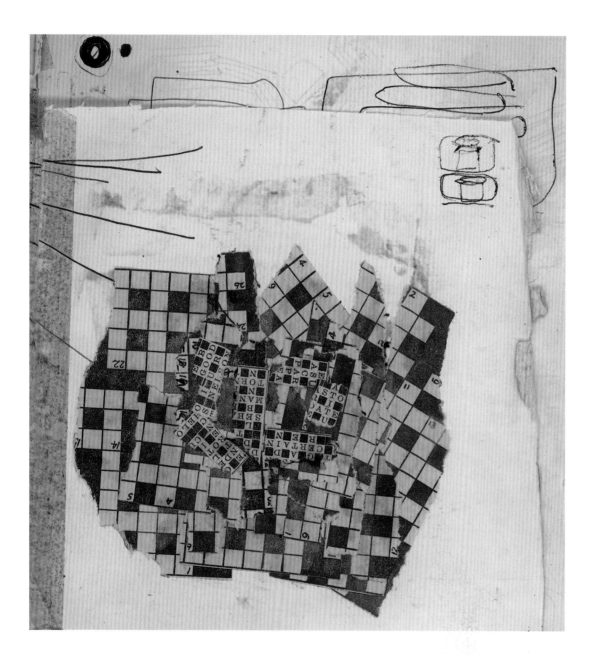

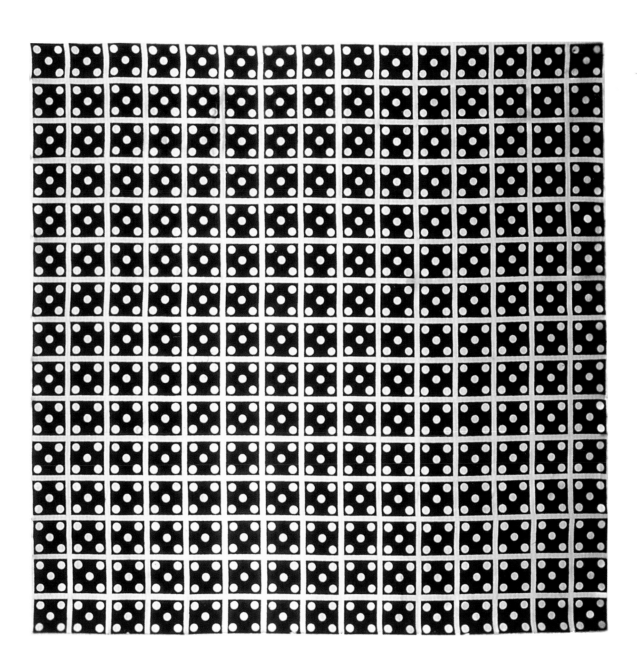

46 Below Pocket design with daffodil and jewel motifs for Angela Sharp, one-colour print on rayon twill, circa 1966.

47/48 Opposite Motif for Angela Sharp, five-colour print on satin, circa 1966.

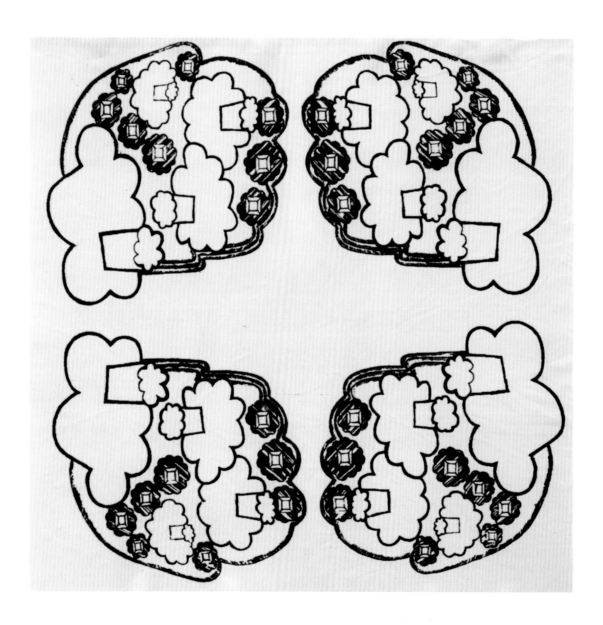

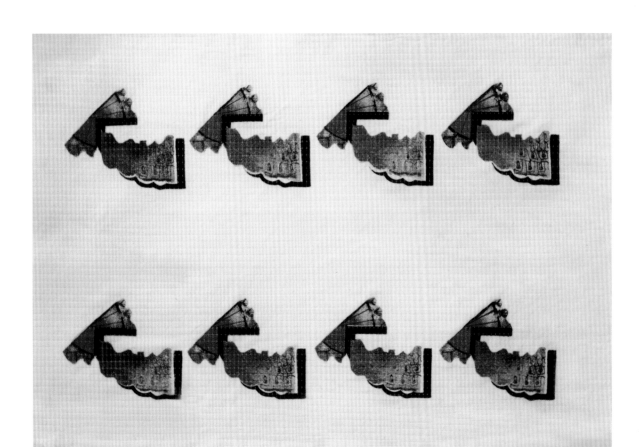

49 Left *Bricks*, four-colour print on calico, Sylvia Ayton and Zandra Rhodes, circa 1967.

50 Right Brick pocket design, five-colour print on calico, for Sylvia Ayton and Zandra Rhodes, circa 1967. This print was also used by the duo to embellish their tailored mini dresses.

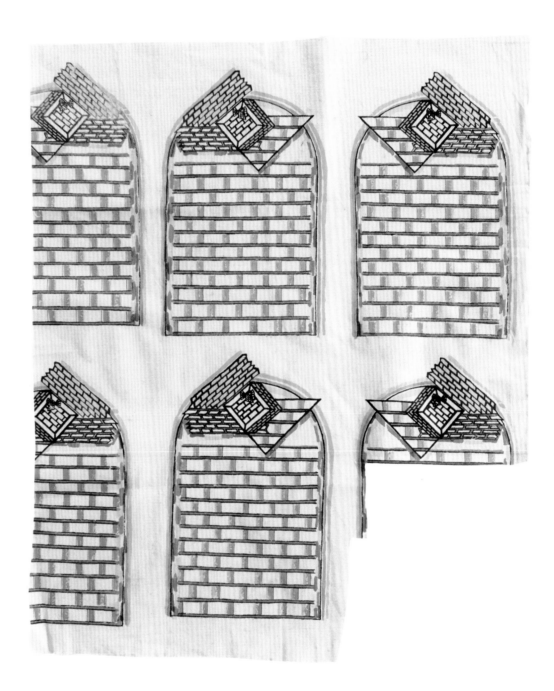

51 *Bricks and Holly*, five-colour print on chiffon, for Sylvia Ayton and Zandra Rhodes, circa 1967. Rhodes and Ayton made scarves out of the print and sent them to their clients and friends as Christmas gifts.

52 Right *Fluorescent Lightbulbs,* three-colour print on paper, for Sylvia Ayton and Zandra Rhodes, 1968. Rhodes and Ayton's paper dress was one of their most commercially successful designs. Molly Parkin featured their paper dress in *Nova*.

53 Opposite *Lightbulbs,* three-colour print on satin, for Sylvia Ayton and Zandra Rhodes, 1967. The print was based on the Blackpool Illuminations and dead fireworks packets found on the ground. Ayton designed a halterneck mini dress with the print, which was featured in *Nova*.

54 Next page *Lightbulb* study on paper using cut out pieces from earlier experiments, 1967.

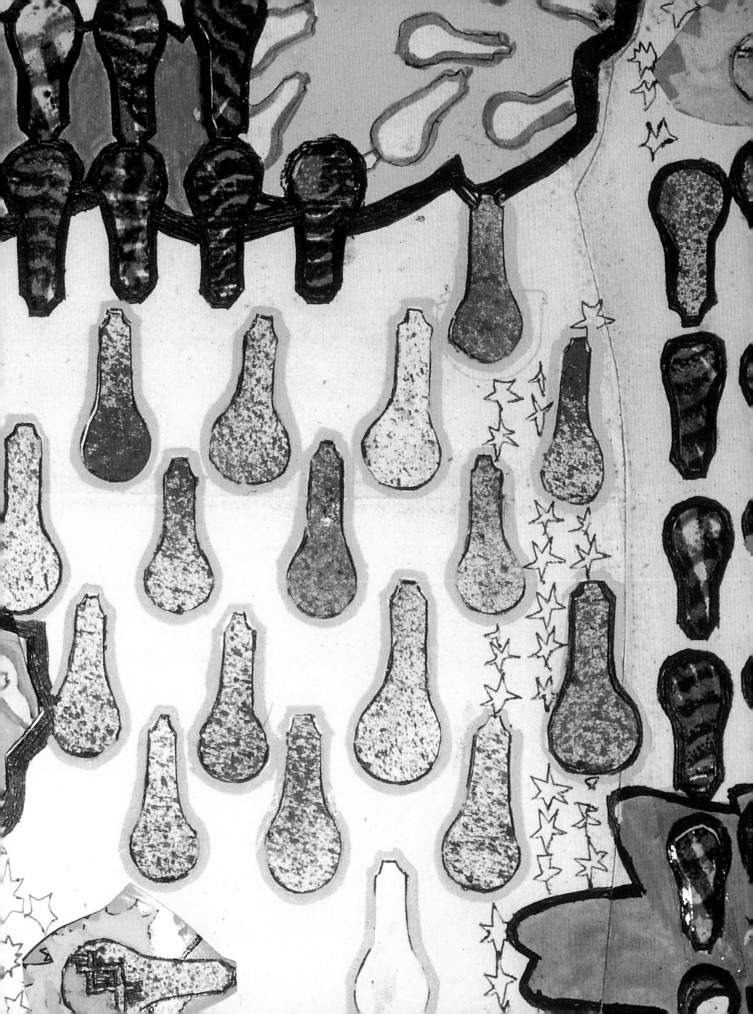

55 *Neon Body Transfers*, Sylvia Ayton and Zandra Rhodes, 1968, sold in Harrods Way In Department.

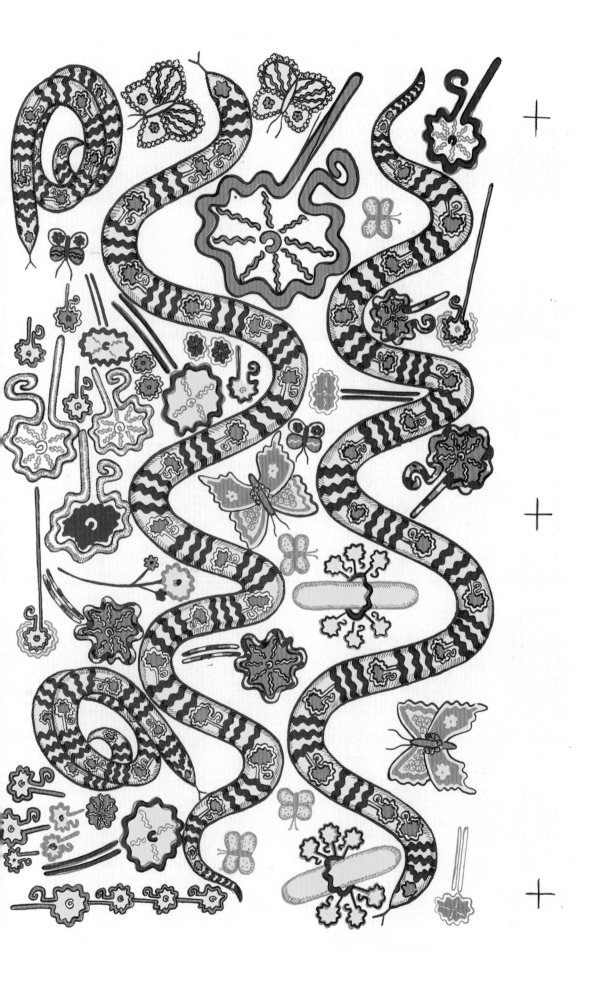

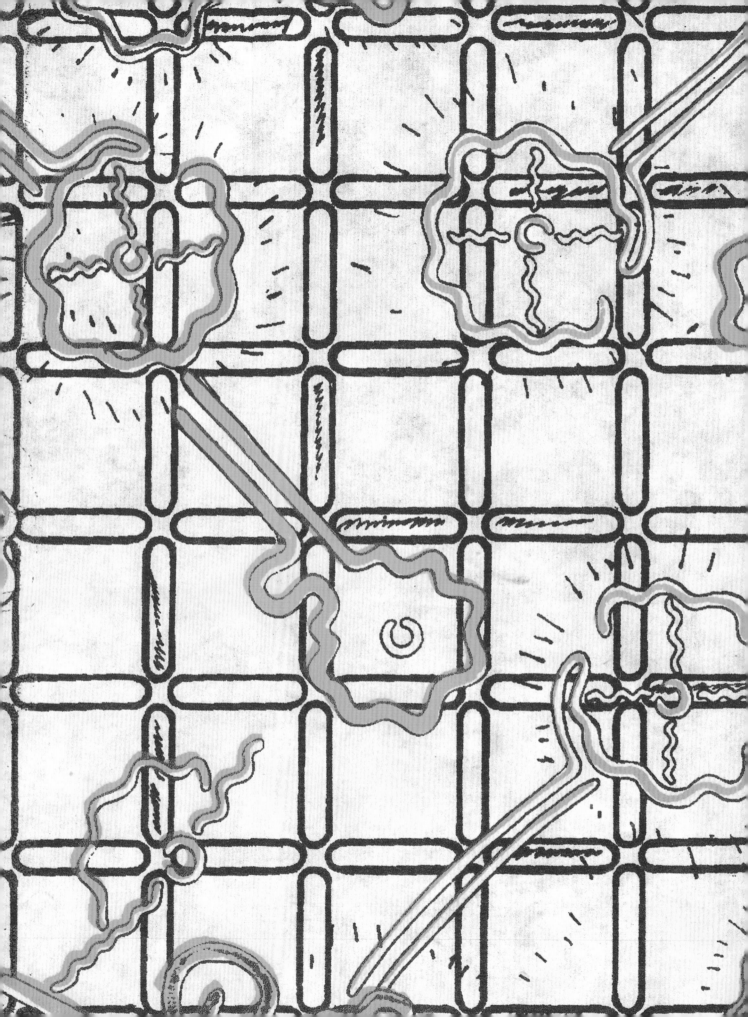

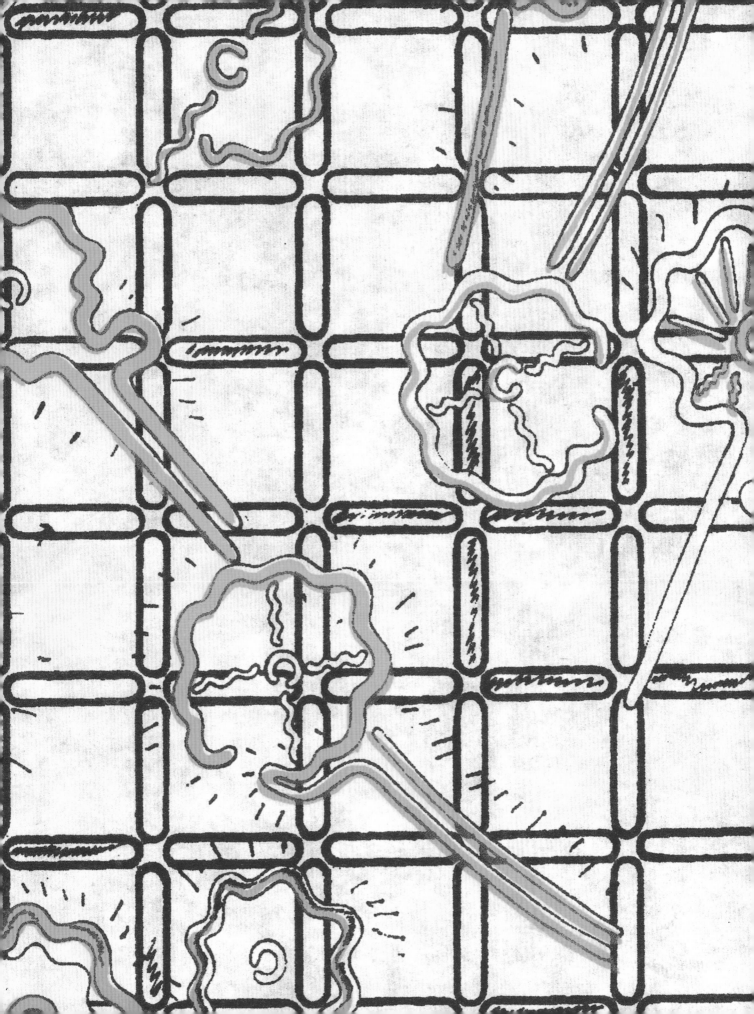

56 Previous spread *Neon Flowers and Grid*, two colour print on paper, Sylvia Ayton and Zandra Rhodes, 1968. This design was hand screen printed on felt and made up into a fetching waistcoat

57 Below left *Neon* design on paper, experimenting with neon flower motifs and neon wiggles, 1968.

58 Below right *Neon Filaments* motif filled with neon flowers, print on paper, 1968.

59 Opposite *Neon Zig Zag Filament* design, three-colour print on paper, 1968, inspired by the live blinking neon lights from the Blackpool illuminations.

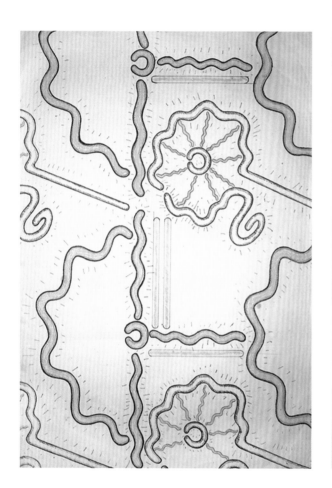

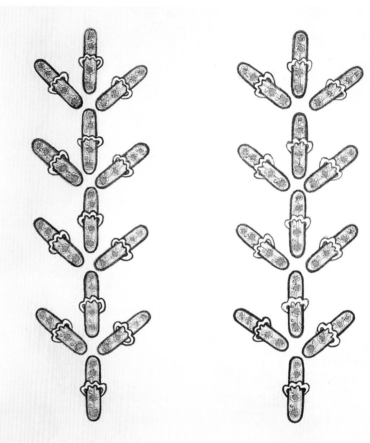

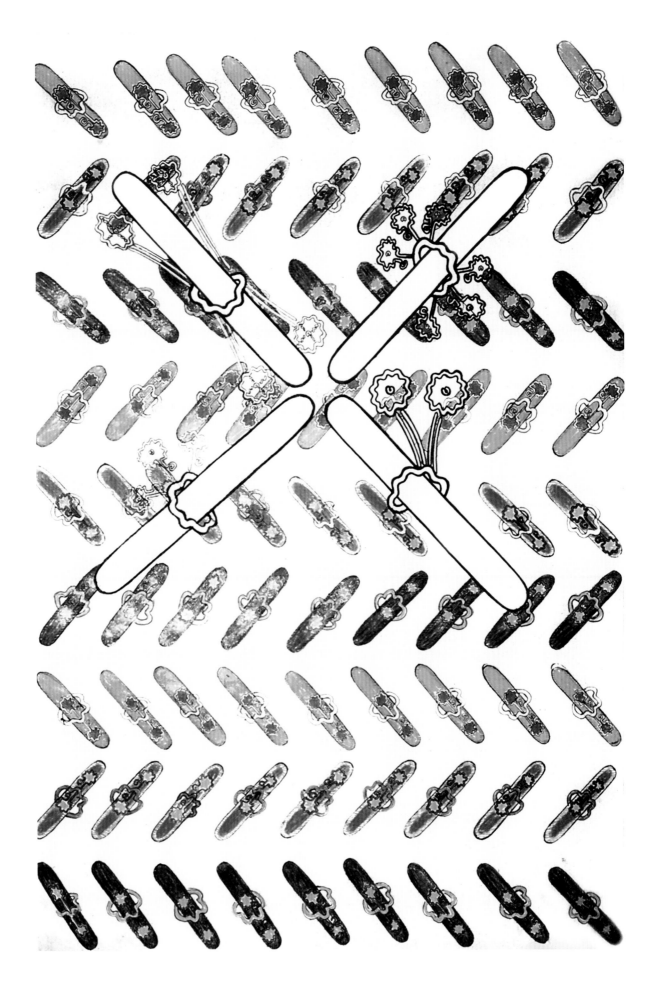

60 *All Over Neon*, three-colour print on jersey, Fulham Road Clothes Shop, 1968.

61 Left *Mr Man*, three-colour print on white rayon crepe, Syliva Ayton and Zandra Rhodes, 1968.

62 Right *Mr Man*, three-colour print on pink rayon crepe, Sylvia Ayton and Zandra Rhodes, 1968. *Mr Man* was inspired by the rainbow-coloured man on the OMO soap packaging and the famous Las Vegas cowboy in neon lights. The print was used for sleeves on a multi-print dress, on a suede jacket as well as a skirt modelled by Vanessa Redgrave in British *Vogue*, June 1968.

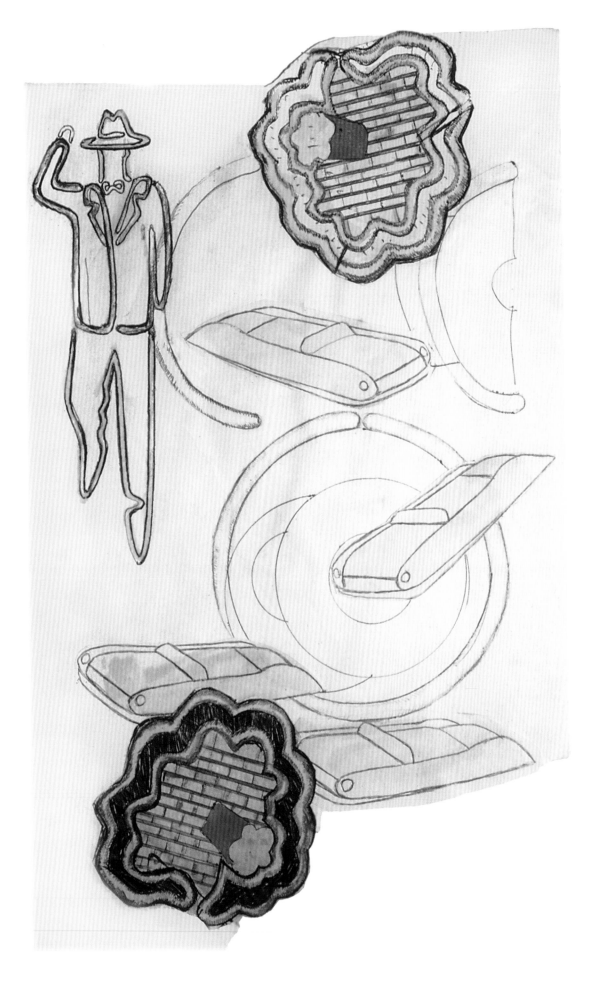

63 **Left** Paper design incorporating *Mr Man* motif, bricks, light filaments and a rendition of Lady Penelope's Rolls Royce from Rhodes's favourite television programme *Thunderbirds*, 1968.

64 **Opposite top** *Lady Penelope Car and Neon Flower design*, two-colour print on double faced pink satin twill, 1968.

65 **Opposite bottom** *Lady Penelope Car and Neon Flower design*, one-colour print on floral flannelette, 1968.

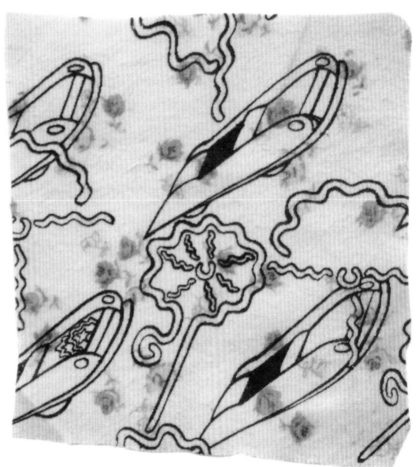

66 Left *Cube* paper idea inspired by Paul Huxley's work in the 1960s using cubes and geometric shapes. Some of the ideas here were used in the final *Zandra Rhodes* wallpaper for Palladio 8, 1968.

67 Right *Cube* yoke for bodice, four-colour print on crepe, Sylvia Ayton and Zandra Rhodes, circa 1966/67.

68 Far right *Zandra*, designed in the early 1960s by Zandra Rhodes, was included in the influential 1968 wallpaper collection, Palladio 8, now housed in the Sanderson archive. Produced in Sanderson's Perivale factory, it was one of the first screen-printed vinyl wallcoverings issued by the Wallpaper Manufacturers' Association.

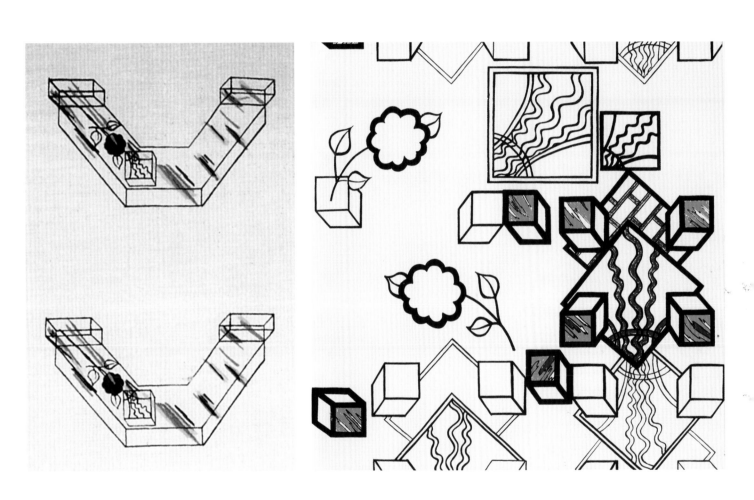

69 Opposite *Hands and Flowers*,
two-colour print on satin, Sylvia
Ayton and Zandra Rhodes, 1968.

70 Above *Hands and Flowers*,
two-colour print on satin,
Sylvia Ayton and Zandra Rhodes,
1968. Inspired by Christian
Dior make-up advertisements
photographed by Guy Bourdin.

71 Left *Hands and Flowers* paper design, 1968.

72 Opposite *Hands and Flowers*, two-colour print on satin, Sylvia Ayton and Zandra Rhodes, 1968.

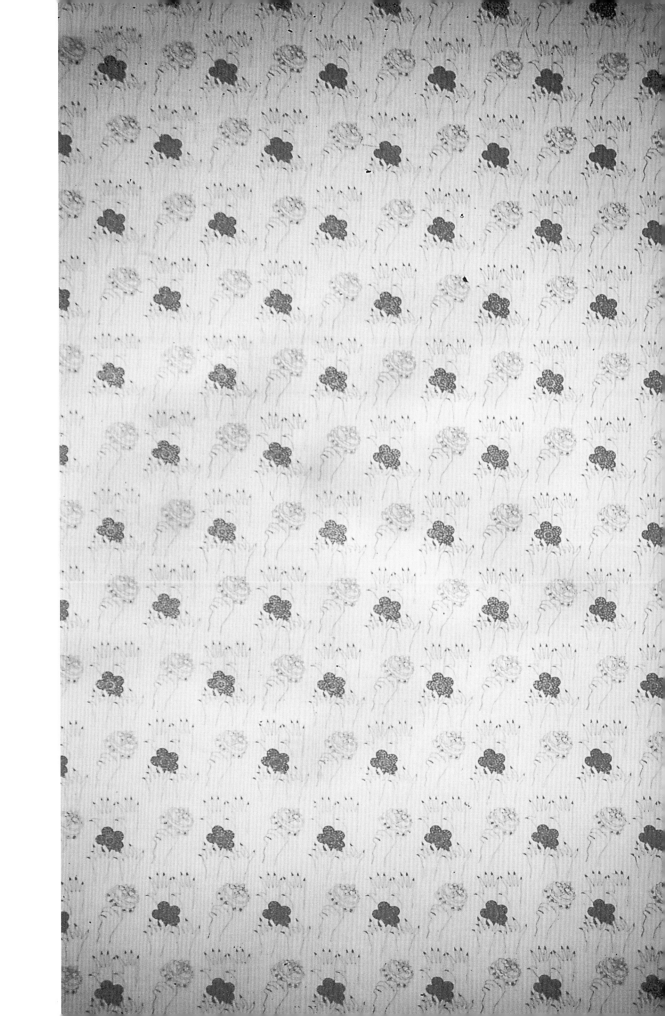

73 Left Section of *Lipsticks*, three-colour print on silk, Sylvia Ayton and Zandra Rhodes, 1968.

74 Right *All-over Lipsticks*, three-colour print on crepe, Sylvia Ayton and Zandra Rhodes, 1968. One of Ayton and Rhodes's most successful prints used for trousers, blouses, and dresses, inspired by Christian Dior beauty advertising.

75/76 *Teddy Bears*, one-colour
print on calico, Sylvia Ayton
and Zandra Rhodes, circa 1967.

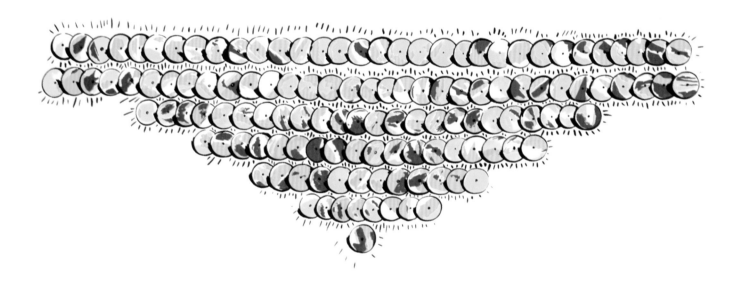

77 *Sequin Bikini*, four-colour print on rayon moiré, Sylvia Ayton and Zandra Rhodes, 1966. The print was inspired by Paco Rabanne's dresses and jewellery fashioned out of phosphorescent Rhodoid plastic discs strung with fine wire. Rhodes and Ayton were photographed for promotional purposes for their label with a model wearing the sequin bikini mini dress.

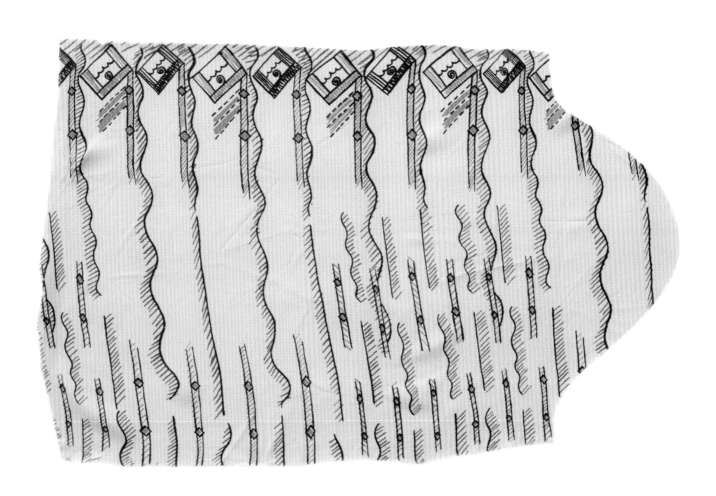

78 *Cross Hatching with Diamond and Roses*, three-colour print on pink crepe, Sylvia Ayton and Zandra Rhodes, 1968. The *Diamond and Roses* print was initially designed when Rhodes was at the RCA, here she amalgamates this motif with her cross hatch designs.

79 Initial sketches for *Wiggle Square*
print in sketchbook, circa 1968-9.

80 *Wiggle Square*, three-colour print on cheese cloth, Fulham Road Clothes Shop, 1968. Rhodes designed the print circa 1966-7 using wiggles, wiggle tassel and neon flower inspired shapes. The print was used in a tiered trouser ensemble shot for *Vogue* May 1969.

81 *Knitted Circle*, three-colour print on silk chiffon, Zandra Rhodes, 1969. This print was made into voluminous felt coats, dresses, and kaftans in various fabrics featured in both British and American *Vogue*. Rhodes's first collection was carried by Fortnum and Mason in London and Henri Bendels in New York City.

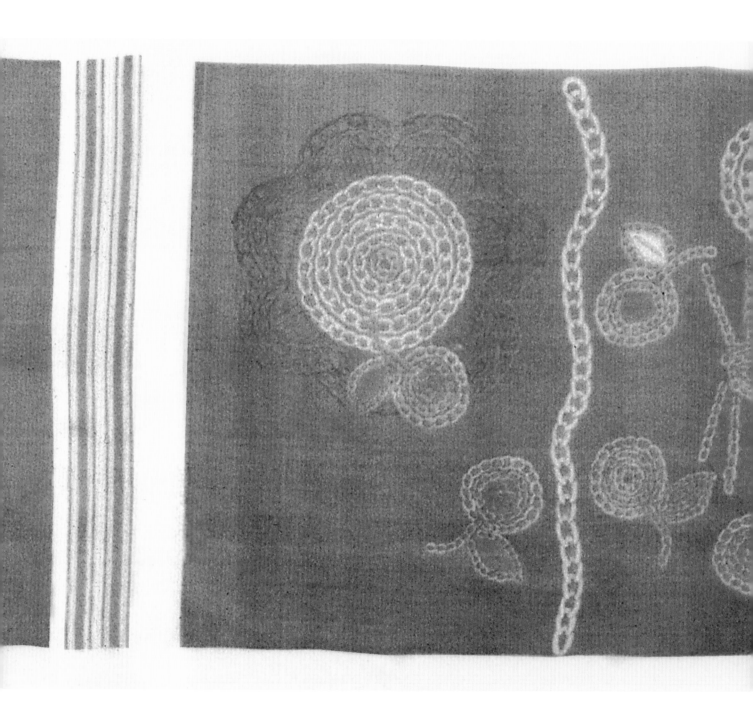

82 *Knitted Landscape*, scarf,
three-colour print on silk
chiffon, Zandra Rhodes, 1969.
The full length of the scarf
has the print reversed.
Rhodes adored this scarf and
could be frequently seen with
it wrapped around her head
in a turban style.

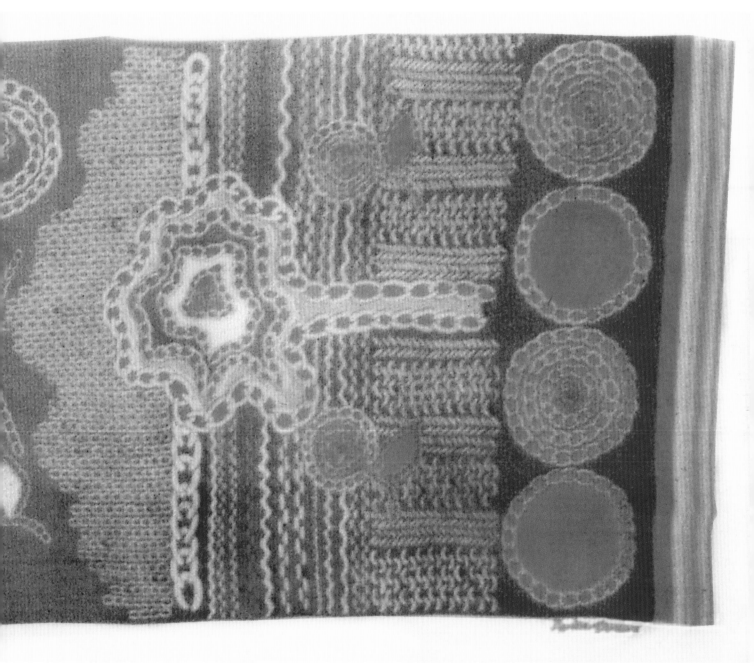

83/84 *Diamond and Roses*,
one-colour print on red and
green poly cotton, Zandra
Rhodes, 1969. Although
Rhodes originally designed
the print whilst at the RCA,
here she simplifies it, only
using one colour.

85 *Diamond and Roses*,
four-colour print on poly
cotton, Zandra Rhodes, 1969.

86 Next page, left *Diamond and Roses*, one-colour print on
yellow poly cotton, Zandra Rhodes, 1969.

87 Next page, right *Diamond and Roses*, scarf, three-colour
print on poly cotton, Zandra Rhodes, 1969. Rhodes originally
designed the print whilst at the RCA.

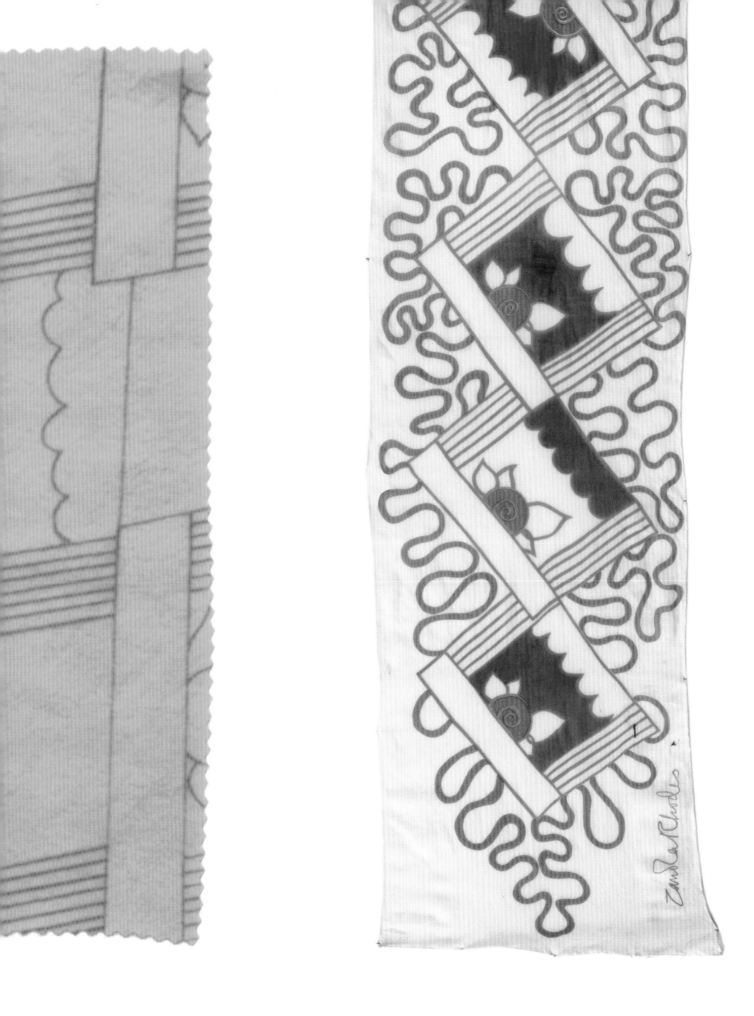

88/89 *Snail Flower and Wiggle
scarf,* three-colour print on
silk twill in two colourways,
Zandra Rhodes for Jacqmar, 1970.

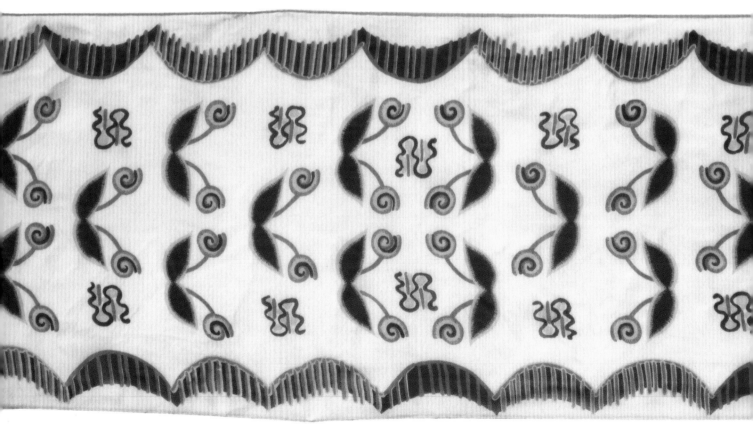

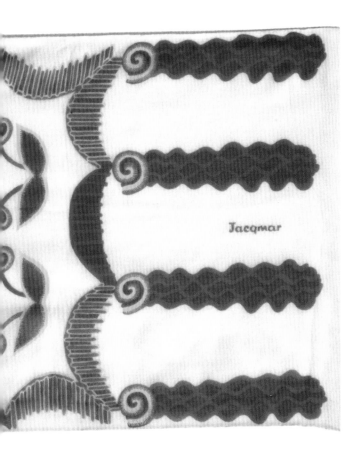

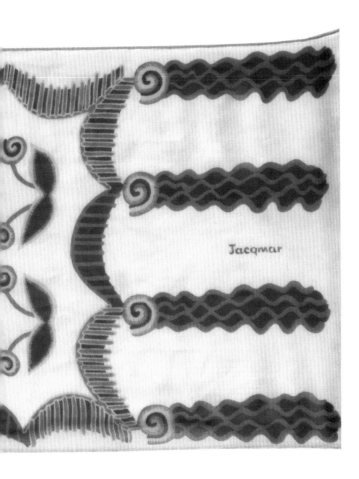

90/91 *Tassels and Flowers
scarf*, three-colour print
on silk chiffon in two
colourways, Zandra Rhodes
for Jacqmar, 1970.

92 Left *Wiggle and Check*, three-colour print on Jacquard satin, Zandra Rhodes, 1970. This design was initially created whilst Rhodes was at the RCA. It was resurrected for the *Chevron Shawl* collection, Rhodes's second solo collection, combined with *Tasseled Circle* in a dress, which was modeled by Penelope Tree in *Vogue* photographed by David Bailey.

93 Right *Wiggle and Check with Tassels scarf*, three-colour print on silk twill, Zandra Rhodes for Jacqmar, 1970. The scarf design includes the key motifs in Rhodes's textiles at the time such as snail flower, wiggle and check, and zigzag tassels.

94 Next page *Tasseled Circle*, three-colour print on cotton sateen, Zandra Rhodes, 1970. This print was designed purely as a circle without interlocking motifs.

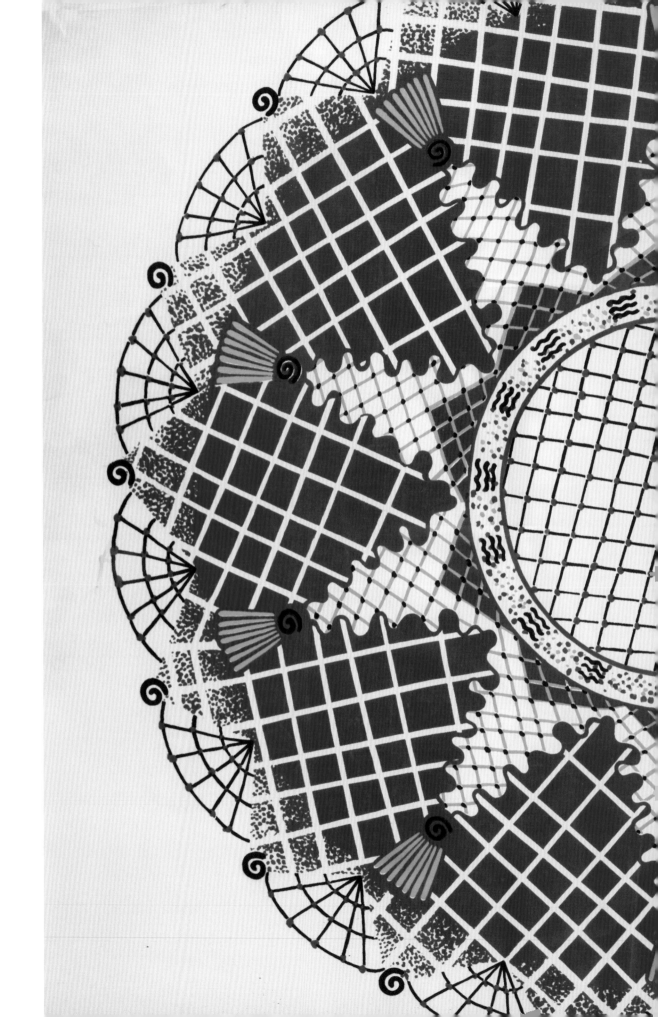

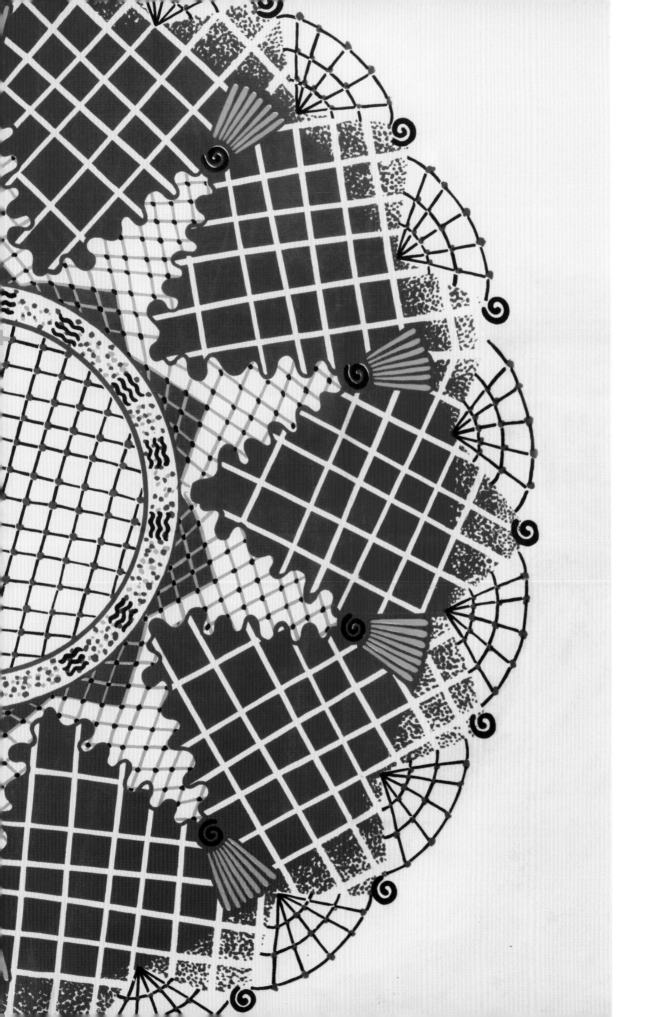

95 Above *Chevron Shawl Print*,
three-colour print on calico,
Zandra Rhodes, 1970.

96 Opposite *Snail Flower and
Wiggle*, five-colour print on
heavy cotton using Rhodes's
signature motifs of wiggles
and snail flower, furnishing
fabric, Zandra Rhodes for
&Vice Versa, 1970

TRIM "TRIPLE POWER FLOWER 65" & VICE VERSA HAND SCREEN PRINT DESIGN BY ZANDRA

97 *Triple Flower Power 65*,
hand screen printed wallpaper,
Zandra Rhodes for &Vice Versa,
1970. The wallpaper measured
27 inches wide and had a 24.75
inch repeat. The wallpaper
came into different mediums,
the vinyl wallcovering was
priced at $14 a roll, the Mylar
wallcovering at $20 a roll,
and the hand screened cotton
textile was $11 a yard.

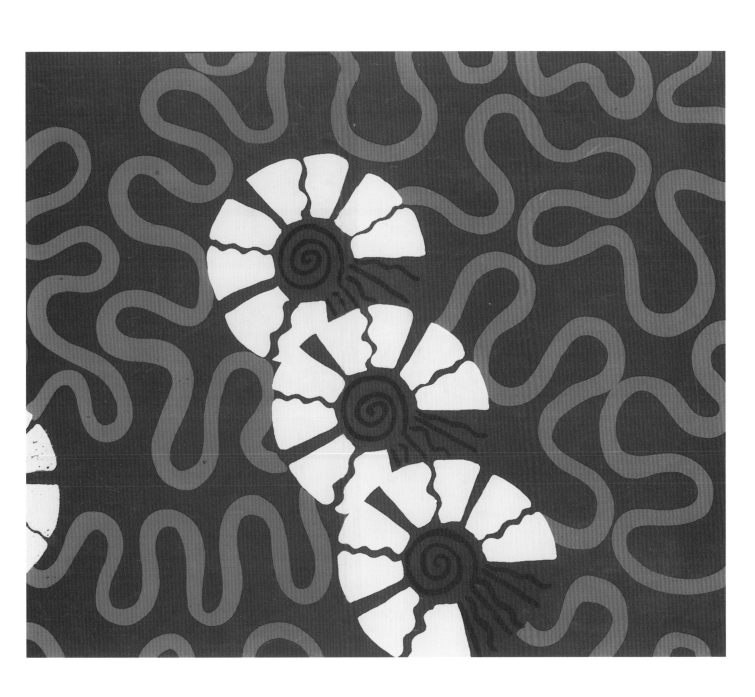

98 *Triple Flower Power 65*,
hand screen printed
wallpaper on Mylar, Zandra
Rhodes for &Vice Versa, 1970

99 *Triple Flower Power 65*,
hand screen printed
wallpaper, Zandra Rhodes
for &Vice Versa, 1970

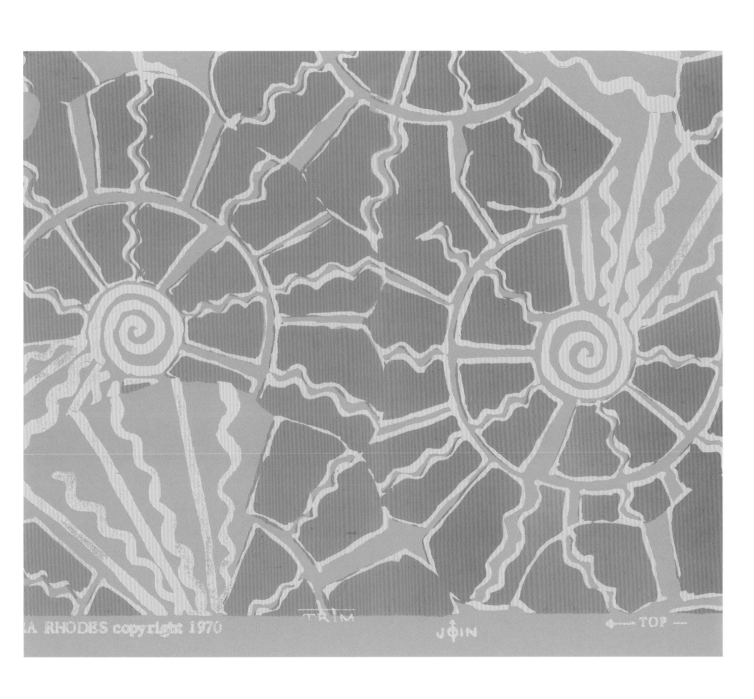

100 *All Over Flower Power*,
hand screen printed
wallpaper on Mylar, Zandra
Rhodes for &Vice Versa, 1970

101 Left *Flower and Tassel*,
hand screen printed wallpaper
on metallic paper, Zandra
Rhodes for &Vice Versa, 1970

102 Above *Leda*, hand screen
printed wallpaper, Zandra
Rhodes for &Vice Versa, 1970.
The vinyl wallcovering was
priced at $13 a roll and the
cotton textile was $12.50 a yard

103 *Swirl*, hand screen printed wallpaper, Zandra Rhodes for &Vice Versa, 1970

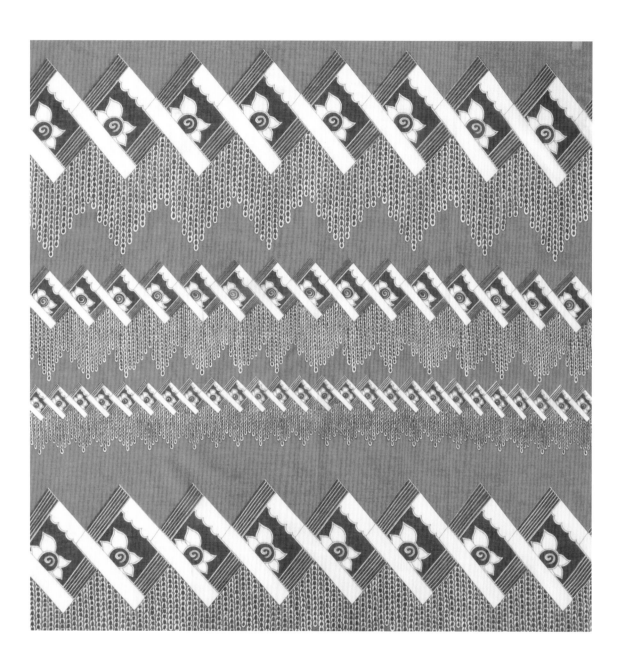

104/105 *Diamond and Roses with Knitted Chains*, three-colour print on poly cotton, Zandra Rhodes for Mafia, 1970.

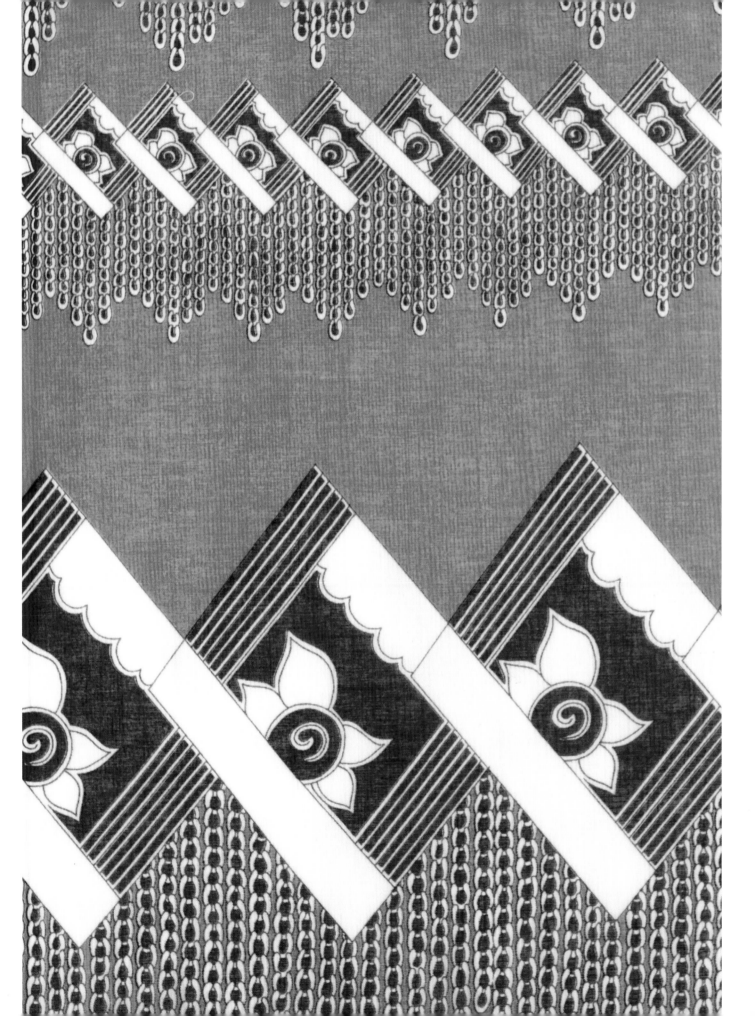

106/107/108 *Diamond and Roses with Knitted Chains*, three-colour print on poly cotton, Zandra Rhodes for Mafia, 1970. This print draws on Rhodes's early design *Diamond and Roses* created at the RCA as well as the knitted chain stitch elements from her first collection *Knitted Circle*.

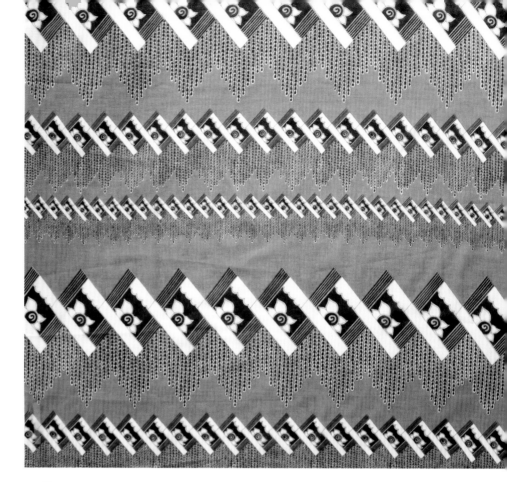

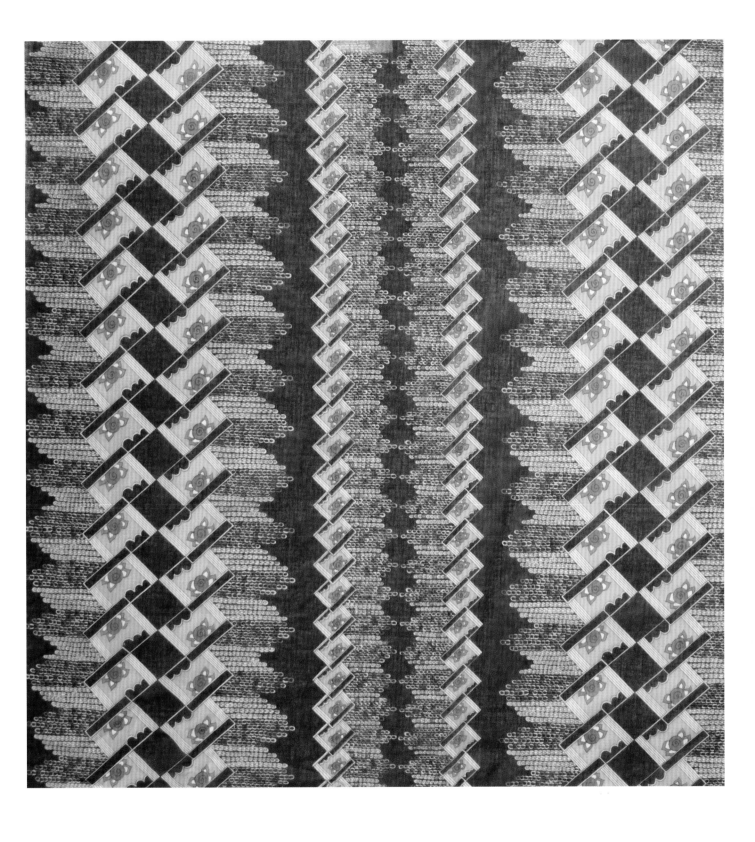

109 *Diamond and Roses with Knitted Chains*, four-colour print on poly cotton, Zandra Rhodes for Mafia, 1970.

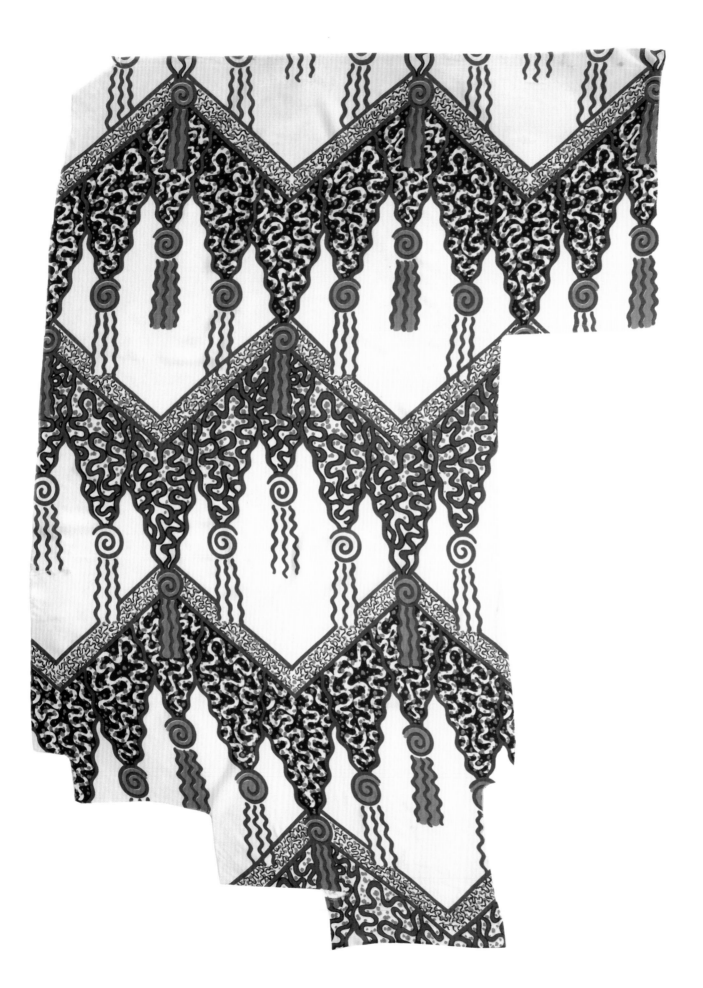

110 Left *Fringed Shawl*,
three-colour print on poly
cotton, Zandra Rhodes
for Mafia, 1970.

111 Right *Fringed Shawl*,
three-colour print on poly
cotton, Zandra Rhodes for
Mafia, 1970. Print is based on
the wiggle fringe and tassels
from the *Chevron Shawl*
print in Rhodes's collection
of the same name, 1970.

112 Previous spread *Mr Man and Cubes*, five-colour print, Zandra Rhodes for Sekers Australia, 1971. Rhodes produced a Pop inspired textile recycling her *Mr Man* motif from 1968 and the cubes from her Palladio 8 wallpaper.

113 Opposite, top *Knitted Flower and Circles*, four-colour print, Zandra Rhodes for Sekers Australia, 1971. The theme of knitting is carried through this textile with knitted circles shaped out of chain stitching taken from the first collection of designs of the same name.

114 Opposite, bottom Logo used on selvedge for Zandra Rhodes's excusive designs for Sekers Australia. This example on *Knitted Flower and Circles*, 1971

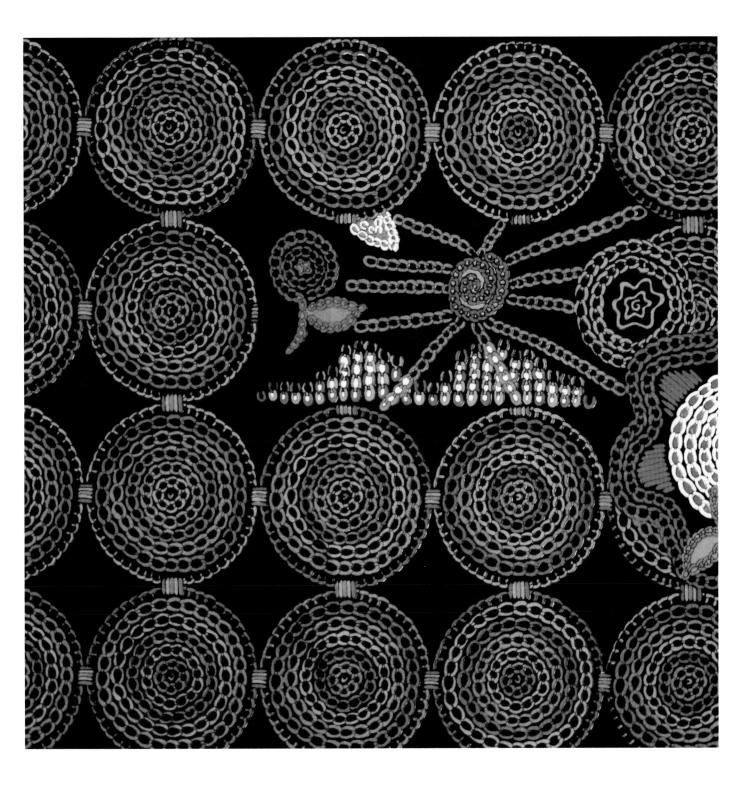

116/117/118 *Knitted Flowers and Wiggles*, four-colour print in three colourways, Zandra Rhodes for Sekers Australia, 1971.

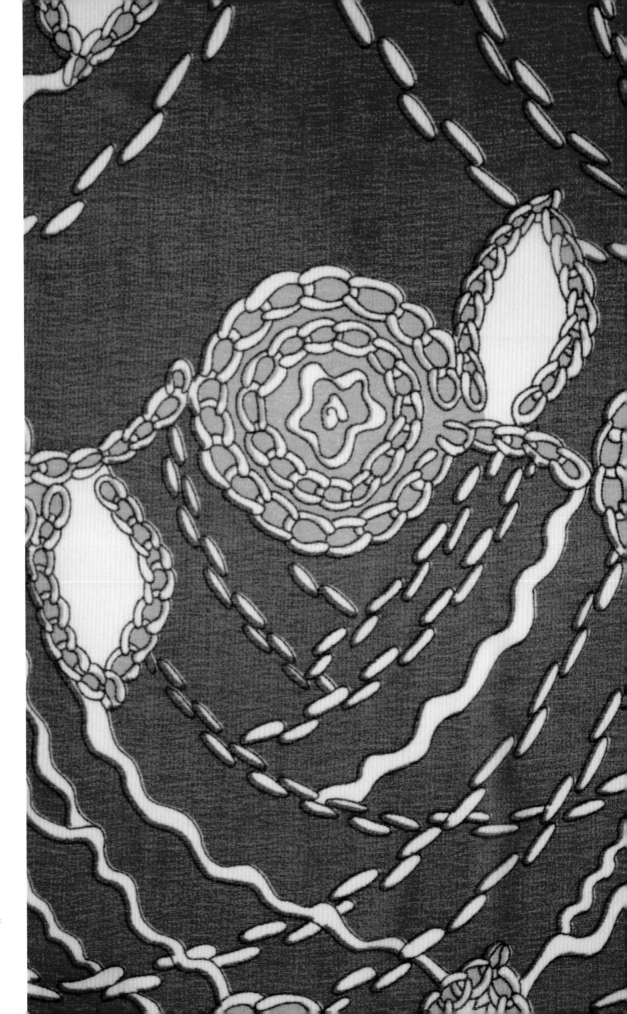

119 Left *Knitted Flowers and Swags*, three-colour print, Zandra Rhodes for Sekers Australia, 1971.

120 Right *Knitted Flowers and Swags*, three-colour print, Zandra Rhodes for Sekers Australia, 1971.

121 *Cross Hatch and Flower Spray*, two-colour print, Zandra Rhodes for Sekers Australia, 1971.

123/124/125 Next page, left *All Over Flower Power 2*, four-colour print shown here in three different colourways, Zandra Rhodes for Sekers Australia, 1971.

126 Next page, right *Flower Power with Wiggle Border*, four-colour print, Zandra Rhodes for Sekers Australia, 1971. Rhodes's well known snail flower motif from the *Chevron Shawl* collection is added here amongst her signature wiggles in the form of a border like stripe throughout the print.

122 *All Over Flower Power 2*, four-colour print, Zandra Rhodes for Sekers Australia, 1971. The print is similar to that designed for &Vice Versa wallpapers, here the wiggles are more pronounced and interesting colourways are used to breathe new life into the textile.

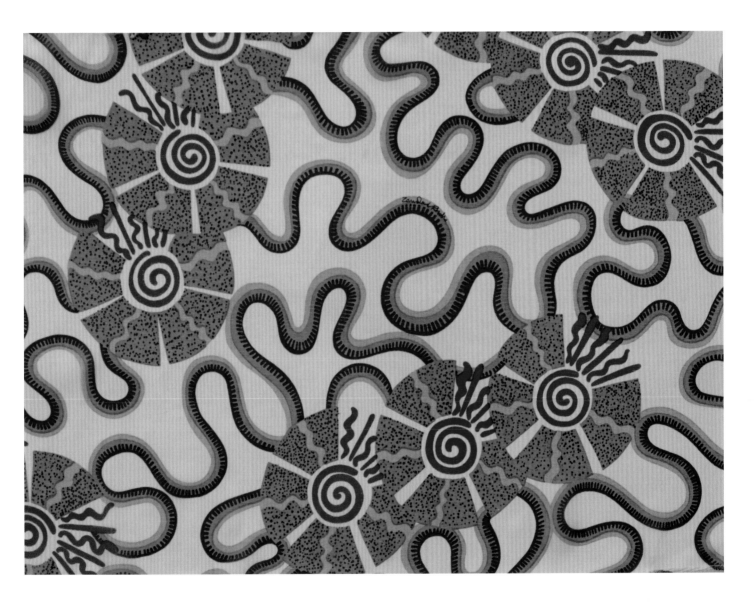

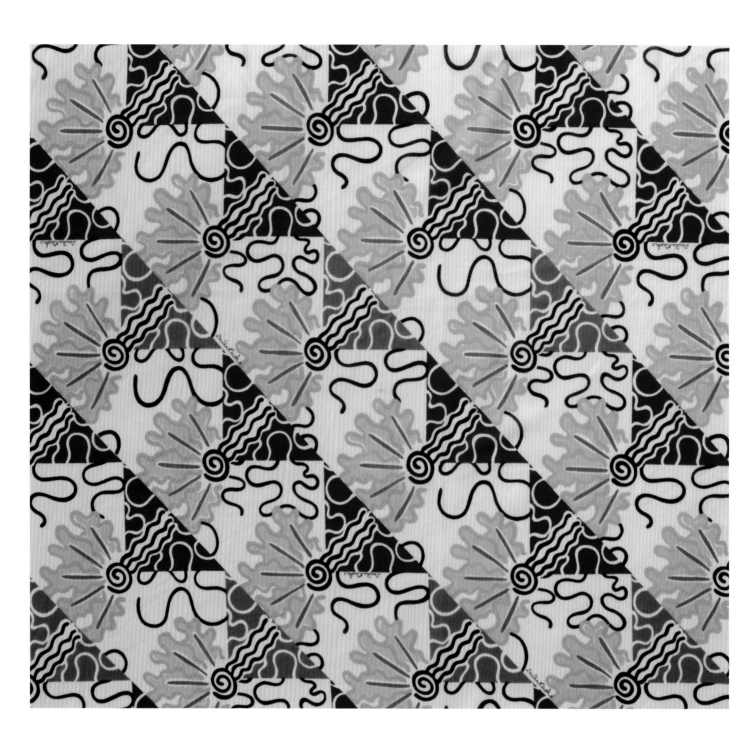

127 Above *Wiggle Tassel Triangle*, five-colour print, Zandra Rhodes for Sekers Australia, 1971.

128 Opposite *Wiggle Tassel Triangle*, five-colour print, Zandra Rhodes for Sekers Australia, 1971.

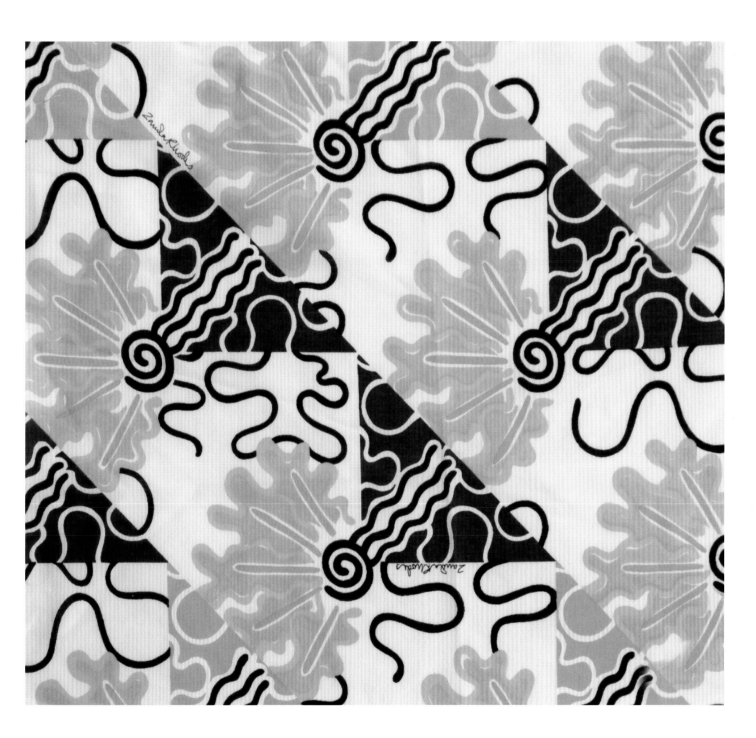

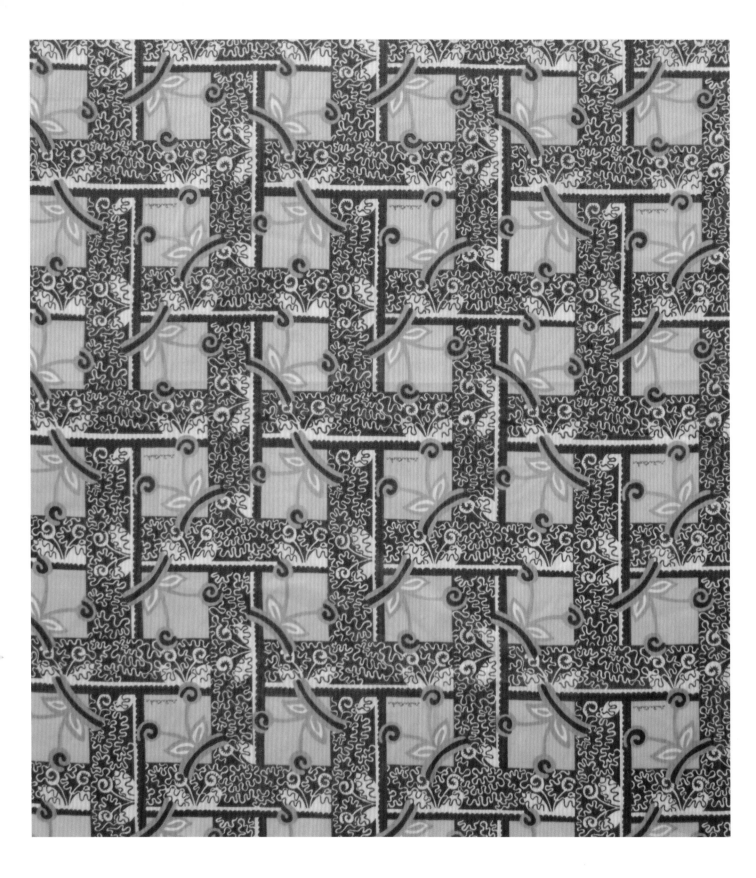

129 Above *Snail Flower Check*,
three-colour print, Zandra
Rhodes for Sekers Australia, 1971.

130/131 Opposite *Snail Flower
Check*, three-colour print,
Zandra Rhodes for Sekers
Australia, 1971.

132/133/134 **Next page** *Flowers and Wiggles Check*,
five-colour print, Zandra Rhodes for Sekers Australia, 1971.

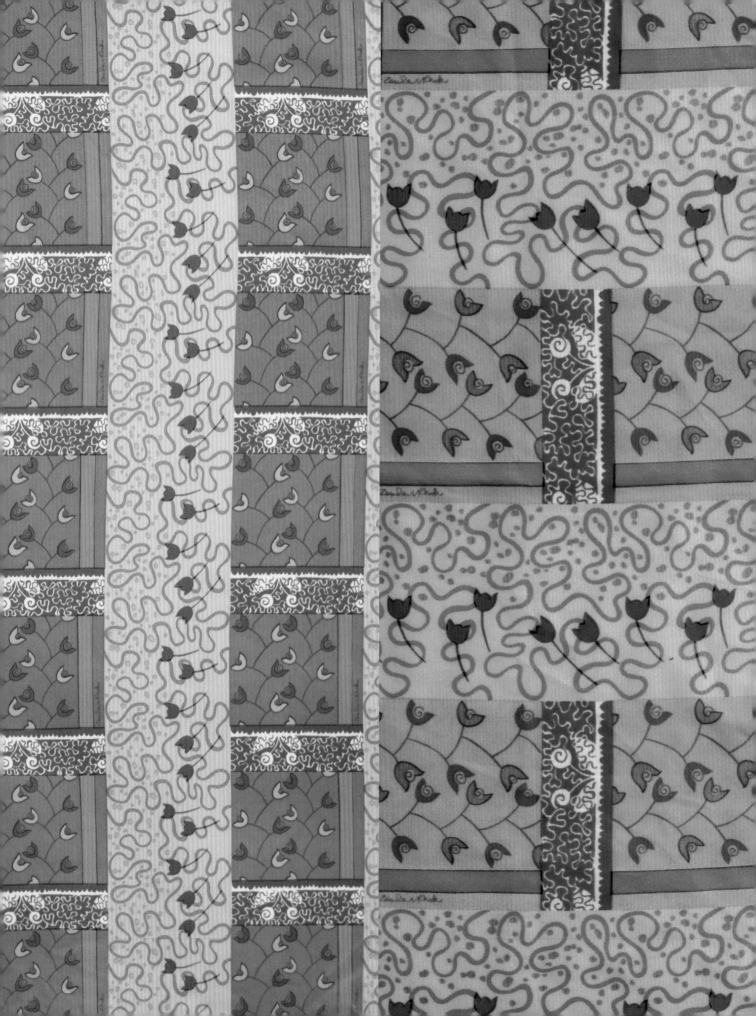

135/136/137 **Previous page** *Wiggle Snail Flower Squares,* four-colour print shown in three colourways, Zandra Rhodes for Sekers Australia, 1971.

138 *Buttonflower,* three-colour print on yellow rayon satin, Zandra Rhodes, 1971.

139 Below *Frilly*, three-colour
print on rayon satin,
Zandra Rhodes, 1971.

140 Opposite *Frilly Flower*,
one-colour print on satin,
Zandra Rhodes, 1971

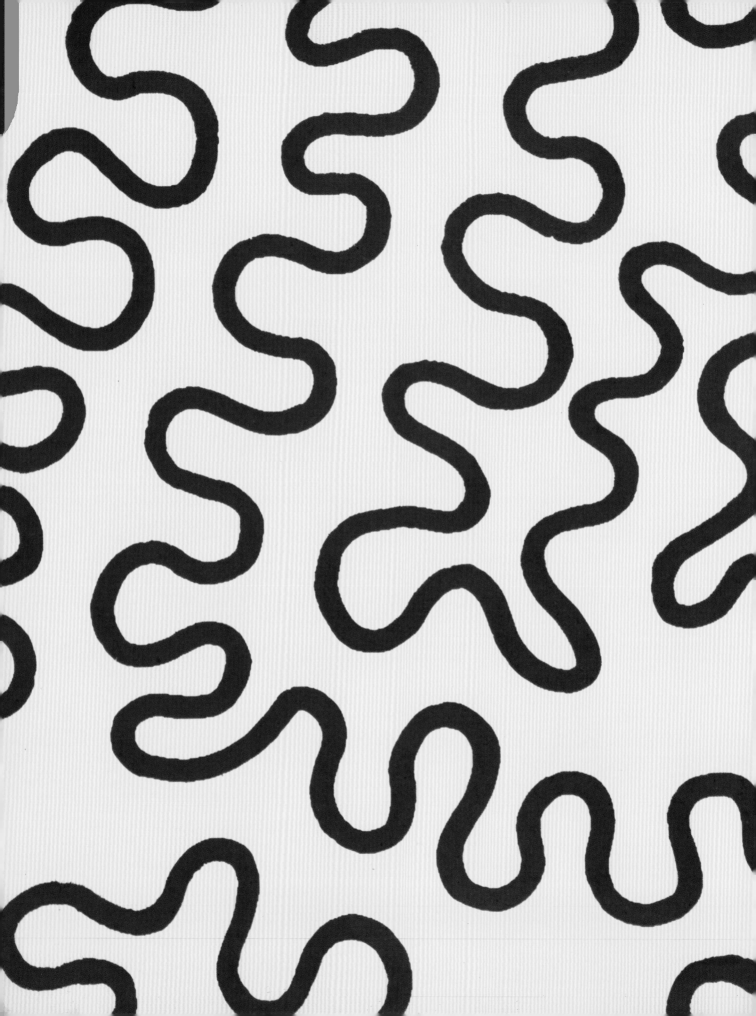

APPENDICES

Awards

1972
Designer of the Year – English Fashion Trade

1974
Royal Designer for Industry (RDI)

1978
Fellow of the Society of Industrial Arts (FSIA)

1979
Best Costume Award for *Romeo and Juliet on Ice* – British Association of Film and Television Emmy Award

1983
Britain's Designer – Clothing and Export Council and the National Economic Development Committee

1985
Alpha Award, Best Show of the Year – Saks Fifth Avenue, New Orleans, Louisiana, U.S.A.

1986
Woman of Distinction Award – Northwood Institute, Dallas, Texas, U.S.A.

1990
Number One Textile Designer in the U.K. – *Observer Magazine*

1991
Alpha Award, Show of the Year – Saks Fifth Avenue, New Orleans, Louisiana, U.S.A.

1995
Hall of Fame Award for outstanding contribution to the British Fashion industry – British Fashion Council

1997
Golden Hanger Award for Lifetime Achievement – Fashion Careers of California College (FCC) San Diego

Commander of the British Empire (CBE)

1998
Leading Woman Entrepreneur of the World – Star Group U.S.A.

Honor Award – National Terrazzo and Mosaic Association Honor for Del Mar Terrace

2002
Pride in Medway Award – The City of Medway, England

2003
Living Legacy Award – San Diego, California

2006
Montblanc Art de la Culture Patronage Award – presented by Sir Christopher Frayling and the Montblanc chairman at The Fashion and Textile Museum.

2007
Honorary Doctorate – Galashields University, Scotland.

Honorary Doctorate – Northhampton University.

2010
Appointed First Chancellor of University of the Creative Arts Kent, England

Exhibitions and Collections

1974
'The Fabric of Pop', Victoria and Albert Museum, London

1978
'Zandra Rhodes', Oriel Gallery, Cardiff, Wales; sponsored by the Welsh Arts Council

1987
Retrospective exhibition, Seibu Seed Hall, Tokyo, Japan

Retrospective exhibition of textiles and garments, Columbus, Ohio, U.S.A.

1989
Exhibition of watercolours, Dyansen Gallery, Los Angeles, California, U.S.A.

1991
Exhibition of watercolours, printed textiles and sketchbooks, Seibu Hall, Tokyo, Japan

1993
'Dressed to Kill', National Gallery of Australia

1994
'Street Chic', Victoria and Albert Museum, London

1996
'100 Years of Royal College Art', London

1997
'Couture to Chaos', Auckland Art Museum, New Zealand

'Punk Kulture', South Melbourne, Australia

'Cutting Edge: Fifty Years of Fashion', Victoria and Albert Museum, London

'The Surface and Beyond', solo exhibition, Victoria and Albert Museum, London

'Best Dressed', Victoria and Albert Museum, London

1998
'The Surface and Beyond', solo exhibition, San Diego

'Costume of the Ancient Egyptians', The Manchester Museum

'Exotisme', Musée de la Mode et du Textile, Paris, France

1999
'5 Personal Garments & All', Museum of Me, London

2000
Exhibition of Magic Flute Sketches', The Museum of Contemporary Art La Jolla

'Way Haute West!', The Museum of Phoenix

'British Designers: From Monarchy to Anarchy', The Museum of Fine Art, Houston

Model of the Fashion & Textile Museum by Ricardo Legorreta, The Royal Academy Summer Exhibition, London

2001
Sayoko, Kobe Museum, Kobe, Japan

'London Fashion', Fashion Institute of Technology, New York

2002
'The BIG, the BOLD, and the BEAUTIFUL', Hand screen-printing for fashion and interiors, Fashion Institute of Technology, New York

2003
Founder of Fashion and Textile Museum, London, England

'My Favourite Dress', Fashion and Textile Museum, London

2004
Key fashion designer featured at special international show in Athens to celebrate the Greek Olympics

2005
'Zandra Rhodes: A Lifelong Love Affair with Textiles', retrospective, Fashion and Textile Museum, London

'Zandra Rhodes: A Lifelong Love Affair with Textiles', Corso Como Milan, Italy

2006
First Grand Fashion Show in the UK for 10 years Spring/Summer 2007 at the Natural History Museum.

Launch of the Zandra Rhodes collection for Royal Doulton china

Harrods International launch of the Zandra Rhodes capsule make-up collection for MAC cosmetics

2007
Collaboration with Topshop for the Zandra Rhodes capsule collection

2009
Launch of Zandra Rhodes Shoes for Strutt Couture

'Pasión por la Moda', retrospective exhibition, Franz Mayer Museum, Mexico City, Mexico

Launch of first collection of printed women's dresses, swimwear, beach bags and underwear with Marks and Spencer, UK

Launch of Zandra Rhodes tableware and bed linen for Marks and Spencer, UK

2010
Launch of camping and colourful outdoor clothing collection for Millets, UK

Launch of the Zandra Rhodes bag collection with Portal Worldwide UK

Launching Zandra Rhodes Bed Linen for Ashley Wilde Ltd UK.

Museum collections

Australia
Museum of Applied Arts and Sciences, Sydney

Canada
Royal Ontario Museum, Toronto

England
Bath Museum of Costume, Bath

City Museum and Art Gallery, Stoke-on-Trent

Fan Museum, London (programme fans)

Fashion and Textile Museum, London

Platt Fields Costume Museum, Manchester

Royal Brighton Pavillion Museum, Brighton

Victoria & Albert Museum, London

France
Musée de la Mode et du Textile, Paris

U.S.A.
Chicago Historical Society, Chicago, Illinois

Phoenix Art Museum, Phoenix, Arizona

Los Angeles County Museum, Los Angeles, California

Metropolitan Museum of Art, New York, New York

Mint Museum, Charlotte, North Carolina

Museum of Contemporary Art San Diego, La Jolla, California

Smithsonian Institution, Washington, D.C.

Opera

2004
The Pearl Fishers – sets and costumes by Zandra Rhodes for San Diego Opera

2005
The Pearl Fishers, New York

The Pearl Fishers, San Francisco Opera

2006
The Magic Flute – costumes by Zandra Rhodes, Dallas, Texas, U.S.A.

2007
Aida – sets and costumes by Zandra Rhodes, opened at English National Opera London, England

2008
The Pearl Fishers – opening at Florida Grand Opera Miami, Florida, U.S.A.

The Pearl Fishers – Washington National Opera, Washington, U.S.A.

Aida – English National Opera (sets and costumes by Zandra Rhodes)

The Pearl Fishers – Opera de Montreal, Montreal, Canada

2009
The Pearl Fishers – sets and costumes designed by Zandra Rhodes, Opera Colorado, Denver

The Pearl Fishers – Minnesota Opera, St. Paul, Minnesota

2010
Aida – sets and costumes by Zandra Rhodes, San Francisco Opera

Bibliography

Books

Brauer, David E. [*et.al*], *Pop art: US/UK connections, 1956-1966*, Houston, Texas, Menil Collection, 2001.

Breward, Christopher, David Gilbert, and Jenny Lister, eds, *Swinging Sixties*, London, V&A Publishing, 2006.

Chapdelaine de Montvalon, Sophie, *Le Beau Pour Tous*, Paris, L'Iconoclaste, 2009.

De La Haye, Amy, ed, *The Cutting Edge: 50 Years of British Fashion 1947-1997*, Woodstock, New York, The Overlook Press, 1997.

Ewing, Elizabeth, *History of Twentieth Century Fashion*, Lanham, Maryland, Barnes & Noble Books, 1974.

Fogg, Marni, *Boutique: A 60s Cultural Phenomenon*, London, Octopus Publishing Group, 2003.

Frankel, Susannah, *Visionaries: Interviews with Fashion Designers*, London, V&A Publications, 2001.

Fraser, Kennedy, *The Fashionable Mind*, New York, Alfred A. Knoff, 1981.

Frayling, Christopher, *Art and Design: 100 Years at the Royal College of Art*, London, Richard Dennis Publications and Collins & Brown, 1999.

Frayling, Christopher and Claire Catterall, *Design of the times: One hundred years of The Royal College of Art*, London, Richard Dennis Publications, 1996.

Hebdige, Dick, *Subculture: The Meaning of Style*, London and New York, Routledge, 1979.

Howell, Georgina, *In Vogue: 75 Years of Style*, Condé Nast Books, 1991.

Ikoku, Ngozi, *British Textile Design From 1940 to the Present*, London, V&A Publications, 1999.

Jackson, Lesley, *20th Century Pattern Design: Textile and Wallpaper Pioneers*, London, Mitchell Beazley, 2002.

Jackson, Lesley, *Shirley Craven and Hull Traders: Revolutionary Fabrics and Furniture 1957-1980*, Woodbridge, Antique Collectors' Club, 2009.

Lobenthal, Joel, *Radical Rags: Fashions of the Sixties*, New York, Abbeville Press Publishers, 1990.

Mellor, David, *The Sixties Art Scene in London*, London, Phaidon, 1993.

Mendes, Valerie, and Amy De La Haye, *20th Century Fashion*, London, Thames and Hudson, 1999.

Morano, Elizabeth, *Sonia Deluanay: Art into Fashion*, foreword by Diana Vreeland, New York, George Braziller, Inc., 1986.

Mulvagh, Jane and Valerie Mendes, *Vogue History of 20th Century Fashion*, London, Viking, 1988.

Polhemus, Ted, *Street Style from Sidewalk to Catwalk*, New York, Thames and Hudson, 1994.

Rennolds Millbank, Caroline, *Couture – The Great Designers*, New York, Stewart, Tabori, and Chang, Inc, 1985.

Rhodes, Zandra, and Anne Knight, *The Art of Zandra Rhodes*, London, Michael O'Mara Books Limited, 1984.

Webb, Iain R, *Foale and Tuffin: The Sixties, A Decade in Fashion*, ACC Editions, 2009.

Magazines and Periodicals

Anan Japan
late 1971

Australian Women's Weekly
30 June 1971
21, 28 July 1971
7, 11, 20 August 1971

Daily Express
1 July 1967
22 May 1969

Daily Telegraph
27 July 1971

Drapers Record
27 July 1968

Evening Post
7 October 1968

Evening Standard
28 April 1972

Harper's Bazaar (British)
April 1969
April 1970

Herald, Melbourne, Australia
7 August 1971

Illustrated London News
October 1978

Nova
April 1967

Observer
25 June 1972

Philadelphia Enquirer
4 May 1971

Queen
December 1964
January 1969
May 1970

Society of Industrial Artists
number 137, London, 1964

Sunday Telegraph Magazine
10 December 1972

Sunday Times
16 June 1968
25 July 1971

Sunday Times Colour Magazine
2 June 1963

Sydney Daily Mirror
17 August 1971

Sydney Sun Herald
15 August 1971

The Times
9 December, 18 August 1969
16 March 1971
25 April 1972
21 August 1973

Vogue, American
October 1969
January, June, September, October 1970

Vogue, British
July 1965
May, June, September, December 1968
January, April, May, December 1969
January, April, June, September, October, November, December 1970
January, March, April, July, September, October, November, December 1971

Vogue, Italian
July/August 1971
February 1974

W magazine
January 1976

Western Advocate, Bathurst, Australia
8 August 1971

Womens Wear Daily
14 December 1966
6 March, 27 August 1969
12 March 1971
23 January, 30 January 1976

The Author

Samantha Erin Safer was Assistant Curator of the Fashion and Textile Museum working on several exhibitions such as *My Favourite Dress*, *Zandra Rhodes: A Life Long Love Affair with Textiles*, *Identity: Celebrating 25 Years of i.D Magazine*, as well as various travelling exhibitions around Europe. She was a contributing author to *Lucile Ltd London* (V&A, 2009) and *Grace Kelly Style* (V&A, 2010), and co-authored *My Favourite Dress* (ACC Editions, 2009). Samantha has a degree in Art History from Bard College, New York as well as two masters degrees: History of Design from the Royal College of Art, and Design Management from the London College of Fashion. Currently she works for the V&A as the Brand Marketing Manager.

General Index

Page numbers in bold type refer to images and/or captions

Index of Designs

Wallpapers